JOURNEY NOT CHOSEN...

DESTINATION NOT KNOWN

JOURNEY NOT CHOSEN...

DESTINATION NOT KNOWN

LIVING WITH BIPOLAR DISORDER

MARY WORTHEN

AUGUST HOUSE PUBLISHERS
LITTLE ROCK

Published 2001 by August House Publishers,
P.O. Box 3223, Little Rock, Arkansas 72203, 501-372-5450.

Printed in the United States of America
10 9 8 7 6 5 4 3 2 1 HB
10 9 8 7 6 5 4 3 2 1 PB

Library of Congress Cataloging-in-Publication Data

Worthen, Mary, 1944-
      Journey not chosen—destination not known : living with bipolar disorder /
Mary Worthen.
          p. cm.
      Includes bibliographical references.
      ISBN 0-87483-648-4 (alk. paper) — ISBN 0-87483-647-6 (pbk. : alk. paper)
      1. Worthen, Kristy—Mental health. 2. Manic-depressive illness—Patients—
Biography. 3. Depression, Mental—Patients—Biography. 4. Manic-depres-
sive illness—Patients—Family relationships.

      RC516.W67 2001
      616.89'5'0092--dc21
      [B]   2001022260

Executive Editor: Ted Parkhurst
Project Editor: Jody McNeese Keene
Cover Artist: Carron Hocut
Cover Photograph: Matt Bradley

The paper used in this publication meets the
minimum requirements of the American National Standard for Information
Sciences—Permanence of Paper for Printed Library Materials,
ANSI Z39.48-1984.

**This book made possible in part by an unrestricted
educational grant from Eli Lilly and Company.**

ACKNOWLEDGMENTS

I wish to thank all my friends who encouraged me to write a book about Kristy's illness in order to help others who are going through the same or a similar situation. Their constant encouragement and strong belief in me gave me the strength and the courage to write about one of the hardest situations that Kristy and I have ever gone through.

I wish to thank Dr. Paula Lynch and Dr. Charles Wood of the Little Rock Community Mental Health Center, who encouraged me to go forward with the writing of the book.

Grateful acknowledgment is made to NIMH (the National Institute of Mental Health), Carol Peckham of Nidus Informational Services Inc. for the information in Chapters Three and Four, and the Treatment Advocacy Center for allowing me to summarize some of their material in explaining bipolar disorder and how families deal with the illness. Thanks also to Career Press and Micki Holliday, author of *Secrets of A Power Presentation,* for letting me use information from that book on the speed of thought patterns in normal conversation.

With deep gratitude and heartfelt thanks I wish to acknowledge Eli Lilly and Company for their belief that our story can make a difference and can help others. Without their belief and kindness I would not have been able to publish the book.

Last but not least, I wish to acknowledge Officer Jill Grimley of the Little Rock Police Department for the important role she played in getting my daughter to the hospital for treatment and for her continuing concern, checking on our progress. Her kindness and encouragement will always be remembered and appreciated.

Dedicated to Kristy, with love.

CONTENTS

	Foreword	9
1	Journey Not Chosen…	11
2	Kristy's Story: The Black Hole of My Racing Thoughts	35
3	Bipolar: What Is It?	43
4	What Can Be Done About It?	51
5	How Bipolar Affects Your Life and Your Loved Ones	57
6	Moving Beyond the Illness	61
7	What I Learned at NAMI	65
8	Educational Materials	
	Mental Illness Fact Sheet	71
	Resources for Help and Information	74
	Mental Health Professions	75
	Other Titles and Certifications	79
9	Glossary	81
10	Resources	105
11	Free Medication Programs	109

FOREWORD

Journey Not Chosen…Destination Not Known chronicles the experiences my daughter Kristy and I have had as we deal with Kristy's bipolar disorder. Kristy is battling the illness; both of us are dealing with the effects it has on us as a family.

The journey has taken us through the abyss of hell with fleeting glimpses of heaven. The depression side of bipolar took her to the deepest lows, causing her to have difficulty functioning properly. The mania side took Kristy to incredible highs, making her believe she was superhuman. When the delusions set in, she firmly believed she was the person or creature her manic mind had created. For seven days, she did not eat or sleep. She paced, she prayed, she cursed; she was gentle, she was violent, she was soft-spoken, she was loud; all depending on what illusion her manic mind had created. She wrote beautiful, heart-rending poems. She painted vivid, spectacular scenes her mind saw in the Bible verses she read. She alternated among being Jesus Christ, God, angels, demons, vampires, and someone she named Persephone.

At last we have been able to get in control of the illness. Kristy takes Zyprexa, the mood-stabilizing medication her doctor has prescribed, along with medications to control her depression. Help from mental-health professionals, out-patient day treatment classes, and support from family and friends has helped us cope with the disorder.

The journey has taught us where and when to get help and that educating ourselves about the illness is the key to getting better. One of the main keys to staying stable is learning to recognize the triggers that can bring on mania or depression and to confront and diffuse the trigger before it brings on a full-blown episode of the illness.

We have learned to move beyond the illness by getting back in the normal routine of life. For instance, Kristy has enrolled in photography classes so that she can become the photographer for magazines, books, and newspapers she has always dreamed about being. By following her doctor's orders, staying on her Zyprexa, and taking an active role in the treatment of her illness, I know Kristy can make her dream of being a photographer become a reality.

Even though there is no cure for bipolar disorder, the journey has taught us we can control the symptoms of the illness with medication and not let bipolar control us or our lives.

Our journey is ongoing, and our destination is not yet known...but as we go, we are gaining more control of the illness and more control of our lives. We are determined to live life to its fullest and to enjoy each day.

We hope our story helps others become more aware of bipolar disorder and how to deal with the illness. For more information about bipolar disorder or to find other educational material for family and friends, please see the Educational Materials chapter at the end of this book. You might also want to visit www.zyprexa.com to learn more about this medication, bipolar disorder, and to obtain additional support materials.

JOURNEY NOT CHOSEN...

I didn't ask for the phone to ring the morning of December 13, 1999, but the ringing of the phone was the start of a journey for my daughter and me that we had not chosen nor would have chosen had we had a choice.

For the next forty-five days, the daughter I knew and loved as Kristy Worthen would not surface again. I would get fleeting glimpses of her, but they were few and far between. Kristy had been slowly changing for the last several weeks, ever since I moved back to Little Rock. She could change moods and personalities before my very eyes, sometimes more than once in the same twenty-four hours, but that was to prove mild compared with the things that would happen in the next seven days.

The ringing phone brought me wide awake. As I looked over to see the clock, my mind was racing: had I overslept? The clock read 6:43 A.M.

I glanced at the Caller I.D. as I grabbed the phone. When I saw it was my daughter Kristy's number, I knew something had to be wrong—Kristy was never a morning person. Unless she had to get up to go to work, she often would sleep until noon or later. I said hello into the phone, and I could hear Kristy's voice saying, "Mom, can you come get me and take me to your house?" Her voice sounded cheerful—almost too cheerful.

I assured her I could and that I would be right over. I asked her if everything was okay. She sounded agitated as she said, "Mom, I'm fine. I just want to spend the day at your house."

I had been worried about her since I moved back to Little Rock in September. I had tried countless times to get her to see a doctor. She would either be depressed and moody, often crying and saying very little, or she would have outbursts of temper and yell at anyone for everything.

She also had quit her job. She had a yelling match with a customer, went home, and did not go back. Since she had quit, things had really deteriorated. Her moods were somber and foreboding.

I would try to pick her up and take her shopping or try to get her to go to lunch with me. Sometimes she would accept the invitations, and when she did, it was not unusual to get to the restaurant or the shopping center only to have her start crying and say she couldn't go in. If we did manage to go in, she would grab my hand and walk close beside me like she had done when she was three or four years old, never letting go of my hand. We would have to get the item we were looking for and leave the store. She couldn't stand being in a crowd.

I pleaded with her to let me take her to a doctor. She always refused. I had even tried to talk with Kristy's boyfriend Michael, who she lived with, about Kristy's actions. He said, "She's just going through some things. She'll be okay." I said, "Don't you think her behavior seems strange?" He said, "What do you mean, strange?" I wanted to shake both of them.

Now she had called at 6:43 A.M. wanting me to pick her up. I was in a panic. I jumped out of bed and pulled on some clothes, grabbed my purse and cell phone, and was starting out the door when the phone rang again.

It was Kristy. She said, "Mom, I decided to walk up to the Mount and visit Dad. I'm just going to stay there and visit him." Her dad and I are divorced, so it is not unusual for her to visit him at his work. The "Mount" is Mount Saint Mary's Academy, the Catholic high school for girls that Kristy attended and graduated from in 1996.

Kristy's dad has worked at the Mount for more than fifteen years, so it is more like a home to Kristy than a school. In the winter, her dad goes in early and unlocks the doors so the girls who get there early can get in out of the cold. The Mount was right across the street from Kristy's apartment.

When she called the first time, Kristy sounded wide awake and somewhat cheerful, which had surprised me. This time her voice had a sing-songy tone to it.

I asked to talk to her dad. I asked him if he thought Kristy was okay. He said, "She looks fine to me, said she just wants to sit and read the Bible and draw." I said, "Dale, doesn't that seem odd to you?" Kristy hadn't been going to Mass for a long time and now all of sudden she had taken a deep interest in reading the Bible.

He said, "I don't know, she seems okay to me." I told him if she changed her mind to call me and I would come get her.

Lately when I had called to talk with Kristy, she would talk about reading the Bible, or she would call me and ask where to find a certain verse. I have a strong faith in God and pray for Kristy on a daily basis, so at first I was excited that she was reading the Bible. When it got to be the focal point of most of our conversations, however, I had a funny feeling that something was wrong. I hoped her renewed interest in the Bible was a turning point in her life. In a way it was, but not the turning point that I had hoped for.

About an hour after I had talked to Dale, the phone rang again. It was Dale, calling from his house. He said, "Mary, you need to come and pick Kristy up. There is something really wrong with her. She was sitting in my office at school reading the Bible, then she started laughing really loudly. Then she fell on the floor crying. I picked her up and took her to my house. She has calmed down some, but you need to come right on over!"

I ran out, jumped in the car, and rushed over to his house. I went in, and she seemed to be calmer than she had been in several days. There was no sign that any crying or emotional outburst had taken place. She seemed to be very lucid and was making normal conversation.

I said, "Honey, don't you think we should go see a doctor? Your dad said you had been reading your Bible and laughing, then you fell on the floor crying."

She was very forceful in making and sticking with her decision not to go to a doctor. Her voice was harsh and firm as she said, "I'm twenty-one years old, you can't tell me what to do!" Then her voice softened and she said, "I just got a little sad, but I'm okay now."

I didn't want to agitate her, so I humored her. "Do you want to go home with me?" She gathered up her Bible and drawing pad, gave her dad a kiss and a hug, and we walked out the door.

I had taken the day off because I had doctors' appointments to have some tests run. One was in the morning, one in the afternoon, and then a doctor's appointment after the tests.

I had called Kristy the day before asking her to go with me to the doctor, hoping that way I could at least get her into a doctor's office. Maybe my doctor could look at her and see if he could tell anything by just observing her.

Also, my friends Judy and Kenny Parker had brought their daughter, who has cancer, to the hospital in Little Rock for surgery. I had hoped to run by the hospital and check on them to see how Jennifer was doing. But with this new development with Kristy, I thought I might cancel everything. It was now around 9:30, and my appointment was at 11:15.

As we were getting in the car, Kristy surprised me by asking, "Mom, do we want to run by the hospital and see about Jennifer and Judy?" Her voice was clear and full of normal concern. I said, "Are you sure you feel up to it?"

We weren't ten minutes from the hospital. We could run over and see how the surgery was going, and I would still have time to take Kristy back to my house if she didn't want to go with me to have my tests run.

At first it seemed like a normal day, just a normal visit to see a friend in the hospital. Kristy either made or joined in on the conversation with me all the way to the hospital. We went in, found the surgery waiting room and talked to my friends. They said they hadn't heard anything yet, that it was probably a little early for the doctors to come out and talk with them. We decided to wait with them a little longer.

I glanced over to where Kristy was sitting, quietly reading her

Bible. After a moment, she started a conversation with another woman sitting next to her. Kristy had always been shy and lately was really reserved, so I was a little shocked to see her talking with a complete stranger. I noticed she started reading her Bible again, and I went back to talking with Judy.

Within a few minutes, Kristy started a shrill, loud laughter. I jumped up, and by the time I got to her, she had fallen on the floor crying and asking God to forgive her. Everyone in the waiting room was aghast to see such a spectacle.

I knew then she was completely out of control. I gathered her up in my arms and finally got her quieted. Judy asked if I needed help getting her to the car. I told her we could make it. I got Kristy out of the waiting room and walked her down the hall. I begged her to let me take her to the emergency room. She said, "I told you earlier, I'm not going to see any damn doctor. Now take me home, or do you want me to walk?" Cursing and using an angry tone of voice was unusual for Kristy. I didn't know what she would do next, and I sure didn't want her to break into a run and leave—which I knew in this state of mind she could and *would* do.

I finally managed to get her in the car, and on the way home I asked her one more time if I could take her to see our family doctor. She grabbed hold of the door handle and screamed at me, "I'll jump out of this car if you mention doctor one more time." I slowed down and promised I wouldn't mention the doctor again, that we would just go home. She seemed to calm down, and we drove home.

My mind was spinning. *How was I going to get her any help if she wouldn't let me take her to the doctor?* When we got home, she went in and got in my bed and before long she was sound asleep.

I kept praying that the whole day was a nightmare, and I would wake up and everything would be normal. The word "normal" was to take on a new meaning in the days to come. The thoughts of what "normal" would become were unimaginable at the time.

It was almost time for my appointment. I thought about canceling it, but then I realized if I went, it would get me out of the house, where Kristy couldn't hear if I used my cell phone to call her doctor. I left the house hoping to God the test wouldn't take long and I would be back before she ever woke up.

On my way to the test I called the doctor's office and explained Kristy's behavior. They asked how old she was. When I told them twenty-one, they said if she refused help there was nothing they could do. I thought, "That is just a nurse speaking; I'll wait and talk directly to the doctor when I see him."

I had the test done and rushed back home. Kristy was still asleep. I made some lunch and woke her up to see if she would eat anything. She woke up and ate part of a garden burger and drank some juice. I told her I had to go for another test and then see the doctor. I asked her if she would go with me to keep me company.

The old Kristy would have made sure she went with me, but this Kristy said, "I want to go back to sleep. Will you hurry up and come home?" Her voice sounded like a little girl's who doesn't want to be separated from her mother. I assured her I would be home as quickly as I could. I told her to sleep until I got back, and if she did wake up, to just watch TV but not to go outside. I made her promise me that she wouldn't.

I waited until she fell asleep, and then I left for my doctors' appointments. When I finally got in to see the doctor, I was more concerned with telling him about Kristy than with why I was there. He told me the same thing the nurse had told me: as long as Kristy refused to see a doctor, I couldn't make her, and that without seeing her, he couldn't prescribe any medication.

We finished my examination, and he said, "I can see how worried you are. I wish I could help but I can't. Maybe you can call some of the counseling centers and see if there is anything they can do."

I rushed home. Kristy was awake and would be for days and nights on end, although I didn't know it then. She was sitting on the couch, balled up with her arms wrapped tightly around her knees and the look of a frightened child on her face. When I walked in, she demanded to know where I had been and why I had been gone so long.

I explained to her I had been to the doctor and that I was home now and wouldn't leave her. She calmed down and wanted to make sure I was okay and wasn't going to get sick and die.

I told her not to worry, I would be just fine. A little later she asked me if she could just stay with me for a few days. I told her that was fine with me, but we should probably call Michael and let him know. She wanted to know if I would call him, because she didn't want to talk to anyone. I waited until I thought Michael would be home from work, then called him. He was agreeable to Kristy staying with me a few days, and said it might do Kristy some good, as he didn't know what to do.

I asked him again if he knew what was wrong. He said, "I don't know. She is just trying to work through some things." I realized that was going to be his standard answer during the rest of this episode. By that time I was frustrated with Michael, worried over Kristy, and feeling helpless because I didn't know *what* to do.

For the rest of the day, Kristy alternated among reading the Bible, laughing, crying, and brief moments of lucidity.

Around 6 P.M. she seemed to stabilize and sat and watched TV with me. She seemed to be a little more alert to her surroundings. She wasn't going to eat dinner, but I talked her into eating a few bites of food and drinking some juice.

After dinner she sat at my desk with her sketch pad. When I asked her what she was doing, she said, "God spoke to me and told me to write the Bible." Then she said, "Maybe God will forgive me if I write the Bible." She had her Bible out and was copying it word for word.

I could tell by her tone of voice that she actually thought she had spoken directly to God, but I still didn't understand that she was delusional. I told her it was time to get ready for bed and she could write more in the morning. She seemed okay with that. She wanted to sleep on the couch, so I told her I would get her some sheets and blankets. I made her bed and then went on to bed myself.

I got up the next morning to find Kristy sitting at the desk writing. The couch looked like no one had even laid on it. I asked her if she had been to bed. She looked at me like she was surprised that I would even ask such a question and said, "I don't have to sleep, and I can't have any more food or anything to drink, and I can't leave God's house until I finish writing the Bible."

I didn't know what to say, so I decided not to say anything.

I spent the day calling every counseling center in Little Rock. I was met with the same final answer each time: since Kristy was twenty-one, had refused to get help, and had not threatened herself or anyone else, there was nothing I could do. It didn't matter how strongly she believed she was seeing God or being told directly by God to write the Bible.

I let my work know I had to take a few days off to take care of Kristy. Her delusions became more pronounced. She firmly believed she was Jesus Christ. As Jesus, she was very soft-spoken, very gentle, but also very intent on writing the Bible. She still had not eaten or drunk anything since Monday night, nor had she slept since she napped on Monday.

I stayed up with her as late as I could on Tuesday night. When I couldn't stay awake any longer, I finally went to bed. I slept some, but mostly tossed and turned, trying to figure out what to do.

On Wednesday I called the state hospital and told them what was happening. I had no idea what was wrong but I knew it was way past anything normal, and I knew nothing I could do was going to make it any better. I got basically the same response I did from the counseling centers and doctors.

They asked me several questions, including, how old is she? Had she ever been in the state hospital before or any other mental institution? Had she threatened to hurt herself or anyone else? Was she willing to come for treatment? I told them she was twenty-one and answered "no" to all the other questions.

They said they were sorry, there was nothing they could do.

Wednesday night Kristy alternated from being Jesus Christ to being an angel to being a demon. As Jesus, she was tender and understanding. As an angel, she was sweet and child-like, doing little dances around the room. As she danced, she held her arms out and said, "Watch me fly." As a demon, she was hostile, argumentative, aggressive, and violent.

Finally, in desperation, I got out the phone book and found a non-emergency number for the police department. I talked to an officer to see if he would come out and help me take her to the hospital. He was very kind and sympathetic, but he, too, said unless she was willing to go to the hospital and she had not done anything wrong, there was nothing he could do.

He asked if she was threatening me or trying to harm me or herself. I told him, "No, she hasn't tried anything like that, but I know she needs to go to a hospital." I broke down crying and hung up.

The night wore on, and I slept off and on. Kristy would come in and wake me up and tell me I needed to get up and sit with her, that she was Jesus, and that I should be sitting beside her while she wrote the Bible.

Around 5:30 or 6 A.M. on Thursday morning, Kristy decided she wanted to go to the convent at Mount Saint Mary's and see Sister Ann. She said the angels had told her that the sisters were expecting her, and I had to take her over there to live with them.

I tried to explain to her it was too early to call over there. Most of the sisters are older nuns, and even though most of them knew Kristy from high school, I wasn't sure they would know what to think seeing her in such a state.

She became very belligerent. She was going whether I liked it or not. She said she was Jesus Christ and the sisters would be glad to see her. She looked me right in the eye and said, "Are you trying to keep me from doing my Father's will?" I said, "No, I just think if we could wait until mid-morning it would be better."

She screamed something at me I didn't understand and went running out of the house. I ran out after her and got her to promise to come back in until I could get my purse and shoes and put on a coat, and then I would take her to the convent.

We got in the car, and Kristy was really revved up. She wanted me to drive faster, did not want me to stop for the red lights, and yelled at me when I would stop for them. She said, "Everyone will understand if you run the damn light; they know I'm Jesus

Christ." One minute she was praying and the next minute she was cursing like a sailor.

I was afraid not to do what she wanted. I couldn't distinguish what exactly I was afraid of if I didn't. I think I was just afraid something would happen before I could figure out how to get her in a medical facility.

I had called the doctor's office late the day before—a Wednesday—and told them she still had not eaten since Monday. They said that eventually she would pass out from lack of food and sleep and at that time I could call 911. But as revved up as she was, it didn't look like Kristy was going to pass out any time soon. She said if I stopped at one more light she would get out and walk. Thank God the next light was green, and after that we were on the freeway.

We flew down the freeway with Kristy's foot on top of mine to make me go faster. I prayed some policeman would see us and pull us over, so he would see that she was in a mental state and take us to the doctor or to jail. Even jail at that moment would have been a relief. At least in jail surely someone could get us the help we needed. I have never been in jail, but if it would have gotten us help I would have gladly gone. At that moment I wasn't sure how much more I could take and keep myself sane.

I finally was able to get to my cell phone. Kristy grabbed it away from me and asked what I was doing. I told her I needed to call her dad, so he could tell the sisters to unlock the front door to the convent so we could get in.

This must have sounded logical to her, because she let me call him. I explained where we were and what was going on and that we were headed to the convent. I asked him to call the sisters. He said he would talk to them and meet me at the convent.

He called me back a little later and said he had talked to Sister Ann, and she was expecting us. Kristy asked who I was talking to. I told her that her dad had called the sisters and they were expecting us. She said, "See, I told you they are waiting for me. They will be glad for me to come."

When I pulled up in front of the convent, Dale was waiting for us. He started toward the car, but before he could get there to open the door for Kristy, she was out of the car like a streak and running up to the convent.

Sister Ann opened the door, gave Kristy a hug, and told her how thin she looked. Kristy said, "I've lost some weight, but I've come to stay with you."

Sister Ann showed us to one of the guest rooms. She asked Kristy if she would like to lie down and rest. Kristy said, "Maybe a little later." Kristy had a backpack with her. She opened it up, took out her Bible, note pads, and pencils and laid them on the desk. She had two of her music boxes, an angel, and her pyramid medicine box.

She sat everything where she wanted it, opened up the closet door, and put her book bag in there, then went around the room moving things here and there, as if straightening up her room at home. Sister Ann told her we would leave her alone and let her get settled. Kristy gave me a hug and told me bye. I hugged her and told her I would see her later.

I followed Sister Ann to the kitchen, where she poured orange juice and talked with Dale and me. She said she would call some of the people she knew and see if we could get Kristy in the hospital, because we had to get help for her somewhere.

I was in total agreement. I told Sister what had been going on all the way up to the moment we got there. When we finished talking, Sister said for me to go on home. She would call the people she knew and would call me with numbers for me to try to get Kristy in a hospital.

As I was leaving, I went back by the room where Kristy was. She looked peaceful and was smiling for the first time in days.

Dale said he would check on her later. I got in the car and left. After I got home, I spent the morning calling the people that Sister Ann had given me numbers for.

Meanwhile, at the convent, Sister Ann was busy making contacts with people she knew. She and Dale were keeping an eye on Kristy. Sister Ann found someone who would see Kristy. Sister Ann told Dale to call me and let me know she would go in and explain to Kristy that we were going to get her some help.

I was on my way to the convent to meet Dale and Sister Ann

to take Kristy up to the doctor when my cell phone rang. It was Dale, who told me Kristy had jumped up and run outside when Sister Ann told her we were going to take her to a doctor. They had lost all trace of her.

When I got there, I suggested we go to her apartment. Michael was home and said Kristy was there, but she was really upset and didn't want to see anyone.

I finally convinced him to let me come inside and talk to her. She was in the bed with all her clothes on and a little knitted cap pulled down over her head and eyes. I asked her if she would get up and come with me. She said that she wouldn't come with me because I didn't believe she was Jesus. She started crying and wanted me to leave.

I told her I would leave, but I would check on her later and for her to call me if she needed me. I talked to Michael and asked him if he realized that Kristy was very sick and that she had no idea who she was or what was going on. He said he did and that if he needed me, he would call me.

I called Michael later that afternoon, and he said after I left, Kristy rested some and then got up and wrote Bible verses and drew pictures using a black marker on the bedroom wall. She wrote:

> WE EARTHDEMONS=UNPROFITABLE SERVANTS
> FOR INDEED THE KINGDOM OF GOD IS WITHIN
> A CERTAIN RULER ASKED HIM, RABBI (good teacher)
>
> WHAT SHALL I DO TO INHERIT ETERNAL LIFE?
> SO JESUS SAID TO HIM, WHY DO YOU CALL
> ME GOOD? NO ONE IS GOOD EXCEPT ONE—GOD.
>
> FATHER, INTO YOUR HANDS I COMMIT MY SPIRIT,
> FOR GOD SO LOVED THE WORLD THAT HE GAVE
> HIS ONLY BEGOTTEN SON, THAT WHOMEVER BELIEVES
> IN HIM SHALL NOT PERISH, BUT HAVE EVERLASTING LIFE.

She had written something similar before at my house and would allude to death. I didn't want to alarm Michael, but I told him to watch her closely.

I called a couple of more times to check on her. Michael always said that Kristy wasn't sleeping, but she would lay down and rest.

On Friday, I checked to see how she was doing again. He said she was taking a shower and seemed to be better, although she still hadn't eaten or slept. She didn't want me to come over, but she said maybe I could come later. Late Friday night, I talked to Michael again. He said she seemed better and he would call me the next day.

I went to bed, only to wake up the next morning to the phone ringing and someone asking me if I was Kristy's mother and if I could come get her.

After I had last talked to Michael, some of their friends had come by and Michael and Kristy went with them. When they got to the house of their friends, there was a young man there that was mentally impaired. Kristy told them since she was Jesus, she could heal him. In her delusional state, she thought she could make him well and refused to go off and leave him.

Since she wouldn't leave with him, Michael left her there. Until I got the call, I thought she was still safe in her apartment.

The person that called gave me the address, and I went and picked Kristy up. She had no idea where or who she was. All that day, the delusions got worse, and the moods cycled from gentle to violent and back again.

On Sunday morning, Kristy took a shower, saying we had to cleanse ourselves and get ready to go to heaven. Around noon she said we could have juice to help cleanse us. She would let me have a small swallow, and then she would take a small swallow. She would say, "Mother first, and I'm second."

As the day wore on, she became someone she called Persephone. She said, "I am Persephone, I perceive with persistence." By late afternoon and early evening, she had us say our prayers and said we would wake up in heaven soon. She would alternate from being Persephone to being Jesus, an angel, a demon, and a vampire.

The moods became more foreboding as night came. I realized that she was talking of death. She said, "Persephone can't take any more pain, death is better than life. Mother will have to sleep first, she can't stand to see the mess."

Kristy closed all the window blinds in the house and unplugged all the phones. She took the phone cords and stacked them with all the phones in a pile on the kitchen cabinet. She took down all of the clocks and took the batteries out of them because, as she said, "Time would be no more." We couldn't open the outside doors anymore, because Kristy said evil was lurking outside and if we opened the door, it would come in and bad things could happen. She told me I would have to be quiet and do what she said because she was Jesus. If I wasn't quiet and didn't do what she said, Jesus would go away and the demon would come.

As Jesus, Kristy would try to reason with herself that death did not have to happen, that death could be overcome, but as a demon and vampire, death was the completion. Death was very real and very near. As Persephone, she knew something bad was going to happen because she "perceived with persistence."

Kristy drew pictures and placed them on the floor in the living room. They were of a young girl with a dagger in her chest and tears dropping from her eyes onto her cheek. The girl in the picture resembled Kristy. She wrote notes about death and placed them on the floor by the picture. Later in the evening, she said she must get her things ready to go to heaven. She was ready to succumb to the Trinity.

She got a plastic art box and put her Bible, note pad, pencils, an angel music box, and some other things she wouldn't let me see inside.

I was scared to death, but so far she had not directly said she was going to hurt herself or me. She would just allude to something that was going to happen and say we would soon be in heaven.

Somewhere between midnight and one A.M. things came to a climax. Kristy said we were now ready to say our prayers, get ready to meet God, and go home to heaven. After we said our prayers, Kristy made me a bed on the couch with clean sheets and lots of pillows. She insisted that I lay there so I could be first to go to heaven, that I must sleep so I could wake up in heaven. As soon as I was in heaven, she said, she would use her box and be in heaven with me in a few minutes. She told me not to be scared, that everything would be over soon. She gave me a hug and a kiss and said she loved me very much. She said God and the angels were waiting for me, and I must sleep now.

She pulled the sheets up over my face and head and said I must sleep so I couldn't see what she had to do next. She said the pictures on the floor had to be completed. I knew she was talking of stabbing herself. She gently lifted my head, tucked the sheets under it, and started pressing on the sheets around my forehead and my eyes. Perhaps she was only doing this to make sure I wouldn't be able to see if she harmed herself. Whatever the reason, I panicked and jumped up.

We scuffled while I tried to get to a phone, plug it in, and dial 911. Just as I finished dialing the number, Kristy jerked the phone cord out of the wall. I didn't talk to anyone, so I wasn't sure if the call had even gone through. Kristy was angry that I had not followed the angels' instructions. She said the angels were gone now and the demon would have to take over.

I tried to get outside, but she got between me and the door, and with some kind of super-strength she kept me from getting outside, despite her eighty-five pound frame. She said I couldn't go outside because evil was there, and bad things could happen to me outside.

We scuffled again. She tried to get me go back to the couch and lay down so we could start all over. Thinking that it might buy me some time, I agreed to go back to the couch, but only if she would let me go through all the prayers again. We had just finished the prayers and I had asked for some juice when we heard a knock on the door. A voice cried, "Open the door, this is the police!"

The knocking and the sound of someone else's voice caught Kristy off guard. I jumped up and ran to the door. Kristy ran right behind me, yelling, "Don't open the door, it's evil trying to get in!" She tried to hold the door closed so the evil couldn't get in, and I tried to pull the door open so the police could save us.

I'm sure those officers had no idea what was taking place on our side of the door, what with all of the yelling and screaming and battling. I finally got the door open a few inches, and the officer stuck a gun barrel in the crack and said, "Open this door now!" I begged, "Please don't shoot, my daughter is very sick." The officer shoved against the door and finally gained entrance into the apartment. She stepped inside with her gun drawn and said in a drill-sergeant voice, "Don't anyone move or say a word. I'm in total control here!"

Those were the best-sounding words I have ever heard. I was so glad to hear someone was in control—because Kristy and I were definitely *out* of control. The situation had long ago spiraled out of any recognition of control.

We were fortunate to have two of the kindest officers I have ever met answer our 911 call. Officer Grimley and Officer King were both very professional, yet kind and considerate. With the situation "under control," the officers could see that Kristy needed medical attention. Officer Grimley then transported us to UAMS Medical Center, where Kristy was observed and later taken to the state hospital, where she would finally be diagnosed as bipolar with manic depressive disorder.

Officer Grimley stayed with us until Kristy was admitted to the state hospital. Somehow, even as sick as Kristy was, she understood that Officer Grimley was there to help and that Officer Grimley was in charge—and in full control. Kristy listened and responded to her faster than she would to me or to the medical staff. Officer Grimley seemed to have a calming effect on Kristy, and I have said many times since that night that sometimes God sends angels dressed in police uniforms. I later wrote a letter to the police department expressing my appreciation to the officers for the professional and compassionate way they handled the call and the situation we were in.

In order for the state hospital to keep Kristy, she would have to be put there by a court order. On December 21, four days before Christmas, I was doing the hardest thing any mother would ever have to do: I was in probate court responding to the questions a judge asked me so they would be able to involuntarily admit and keep my daughter in the state hospital.

As I sat there before answering, a thousand thoughts ran through my mind: *If I tell them the truth, they are sure to keep her. This is my baby, even though she is twenty-one years old. This is the child I love enough to give up my own life for and almost did.* Could I answer those questions that would change her life, that would give her the stigma of being locked in a state hospital, branded as a "mental patient" by our family, our friends, and society? Maybe if I just got up and took her home right now everything would be okay. After all, she looked pretty calm. But I knew in my heart the calmness was the medication they had given her to calm her, and that if we were ever going to get the help we needed to get her well, I had to answer the questions truthfully.

I swallowed hard and answered the tough questions the judge asked. The judge was kind and compassionate; it only took a few minutes. When Kristy was asked if she had anything to say, in her still delusional state, she held up a piece of paper on which she had scribbled the words, "I have the right to remain silent." Her attorney was then asked if he had anything to add. He looked with compassion on the little girl sitting next to him, and in a choked voice answered, "No." The hearing was over. Kristy had been involuntarily admitted to the state hospital and would now start receiving the help she needed.

The state hospital was not the horror story it's often portrayed to be. Kristy was treated with respect, dignity, and kindness and got excellent medical care. The staff saved her life and helped get her back on track. The hospital admitted a young woman who was starving herself, delusional, and suicidal. It gave me back a young lady who knows how to cope with an illness, wants to finish her education, and go on to be a photographer and an artist. It gave me back my daughter. It gave me hope.

Many people have asked me why I went so far before I called 911. It's simple: I had talked to doctors, counseling centers, the state hospital, and the police, and everyone told me that until I could prove she'd threatened to hurt herself or someone else, I could not dial 911. If I called 911 and couldn't prove what I said, it would be my word against hers, and they would have to let Kristy go if she refused help. I knew if that happened, if Kristy got mad and left my house, there was no telling where she would go or what would happen to her. I knew we were at the point that something was going to take place that would prove to everyone Kristy desperately needed help. Up until just moments before I dialed 911, there had been no physical contact and no direct threat, but once she pulled that sheet up over my head I knew I was in real danger.

Long before that moment I had a gut feeling that she was talking suicide, that she had walked as far in the abyss of hell—this overpowering illness—as she could go. As a mother, my desire was to help her get the help she needed, and whatever danger it put me in until I could actually dial 911, I was willing to accept. To get Kristy the help that she finally received has been worth it all.

I understand the legalities and the concerns of the system—not wanting family and friends to be able to put patients involuntarily in mental wards—but there needs to be some way of getting help without having to go to the lengths I did to get loved ones the help they need.

Looking back, I'm sure a lot of the things Kristy went through growing up were part of the bipolar disorder. Though not diagnosed, this powerful illness probably started when she was fourteen. She turned fourteen in February, and like most fourteen-year-olds, she was trying to grow up and find herself, and like most mothers, I worried about her and wanted only the best for her.

Before the summer she was fourteen, she had been an easy child to raise. She was very beautiful, with the largest blue eyes you've ever seen. People would stop us on the street or in stores and compliment her, tell us how beautiful she was. They had done this since she was little, but Kristy never took it too seriously. She never let it go to her head and always remained sweet and polite.

She always did what she was asked to do around the house, worked hard in school, and got good grades. She was very artistic;

she had a natural talent for art and took art classes in school to enhance those skills. She attended church with me on a regular basis. Everyone loved her and always talked about how sweet and talented she was. My other children were grown and gone from home, living in towns several hours away, and my marriage had ended in divorce, but Kristy was the stabilizing factor in my day-to-day life.

Kristy is the youngest of four children, eight years younger than the brother closest to her in age, almost fourteen years younger than her next older brother, and sixteen years younger than her older sister. Our family life had been full of ups and downs. I had heart problems and had been in and out of hospitals with chest pains and finally had to have heart surgery. Her brother, Kenny, had his left lung out when he was fourteen. Her dad and I had a tumultuous marriage with one episode after another, finally ending in divorce. To say the least it had not been an ideal childhood.

I tried hard to protect her from those ups and downs, but working full-time and trying to keep a strained marriage and family together made it hard to cover all the bases. I was to find out later there were things happening I didn't even know about that I should have been protecting her from.

The summer after she turned fourteen, Kristy started running around with a group of people who were not responsible and stayed in trouble with their families and the law. She had been in an automobile accident with some of those friends and was thrown from the car. The doctors found very little wrong with her, and except for minor scrapes and bruises, she seemed okay.

Beginning with that episode, however, I noticed amazing changes in her behavior. Could the stress of being in the wreck or the jolt from being ejected onto the pavement have activated a chemical reaction in her brain that brought on the bipolar?

Where had the help been back then? What could I have done differently that would have gotten her the help she needed? She switched moods often, from a high mood, when she would tell me these were her friends, that she wanted to be with them, that they were her family and I was mean to her, to a depressed mood, when she would say she was sorry for all the problems she was causing, cling to me, cry, and tell me how much she loved me. It seemed like she was always fighting a raging battle from within. She complained of headaches, stomachaches, and backaches.

I took her to doctor after doctor. I had her tested for drugs more times than I care to remember, but they all came back negative. I took her to counselor after counselor and sat there in despair as she refused to cooperate, communicate, or even acknowledge she had a problem. My heart broke time after time as I watched her, helplessly, go from highs to lows, from being sweet and gentle to being aggressive and violent, only to start the cycle all over again.

She managed to graduate from high school, and with only one brush with the law, managed to stay out of any major trouble. That in itself was a miracle, considering her unstable condition and the crowd she ran with. I knew something was wrong but I had no idea what, and I couldn't find anyone who did.

Over the years, Kristy was diagnosed with nervous stomach disorder, anxiety disorder, and mild depression. Most of the doctors assured me that this was normal for teenagers to go through. If they did prescribe medication, Kristy either did not take it or would stop within a day or two, saying her friends said that was not what she needed. She refused to go to counseling.

Some days I held her in my arms and listened as she told me how much she loved me. I saw the gentle side of her as she did all the normal things she used to do. Some days I would see her be so violent she would ram her fist through glass, breaking all the windows in the house. In her junior and senior years of high school, she used drugs and alcohol frequently. I later learned in NAMI classes that many people with mental illness use drugs and alcohol as a coping mechanism, as a subconscious attempt to self-medicate. As Kristy later realized during treatment, the drugs and alcohol were just covering up the problem, not solving it. She also had an eating disorder that she would not admit to.

Of all the diagnoses we were given, no doctor ever mentioned the words bipolar or manic depression. When the state hospital told me that Kristy was bipolar, I had to ask them to explain it.

After the diagnosis, I started looking for books and articles on bipolar. I found very little not written entirely for doctors. I began to wonder how many other parents were like myself, wondering how to get help. How many other parents had given up, not even knowing their child had a mental instability, thinking that the highs and lows were just part of the growing-up process?

Had they tired of coping with the ups and downs, the traumas, the outbursts of anger, the roller coaster of emotions? Did they think their child was on drugs or just being rebellious? How many bipolar people are there who are being wrongly diagnosed?

If you are having problems with your child, and your doctors can't seem to make a diagnosis, ask the doctor straight out if the diagnosis could be bipolar. Some doctors may be reluctant to tell parents their child has a mental illness.

Maybe you don't want to think your child has a mental illness, either. After all, what will your friends think? What will the people you work with and go to church with think? What will the rest of your family think?

What does it matter what "they" think if you can help your child find a way out of the hell he or she is living in?

If your friends and family really care about you, they will stand beside you and support you. If they are not your true friends and family, you don't need them to clutter up your mind. You will have to have all your energies to help your family member live with bipolar.

None of us want to think our child or our family member has a mental illness, but it is better to face it head-on than to try to pretend it isn't there. It is not a disgrace to have a mental illness, but it is a disgrace to try to cover it up and not get help for it.

We have just embarked on this journey, and our destination is not known, but finally at last I feel we have a path to follow. Kristy is still fragile. Her medications still have to be monitored; they make her sleep more; they cause her to gain weight. But more importantly, she is not delusional, and she is beginning to even out in her thinking and rationality.

Her moods have stabilized somewhat, and her rapid speech has changed back to almost normal speech patterns. If anything, due to the medication she is taking, her speech is a littler slower than normal.

She no longer rhymes her words, and she talks of going back to school and getting a job. She has had great care and doctors that believed in her, helped her to understand her illness, and taught her to work *with* the illness instead of *against* it. The doctors and staff at the state hospital as well as the doctors and staff at the Little Rock Community Mental Health Center have been very professional, yet caring and thoughtful and have treated her with respect and dignity.

When we first got Kristy admitted to the state hospital, we had just been through a harrowing experience, and like any mother, all I wanted to know was how soon she would be well and how quickly she could come home. I wanted someone to tell me this nightmare of an experience would soon be over, that they could do a "miracle cure" and Kristy could go home in a few days. I wanted them to say our life would go back to "normal," and we would *never* go through any of this again.

Instead what they told me was sometimes they can get patients out of their delusions in a few days, or it may take a couple of weeks. Sometimes it takes even longer, and sometimes they can't get them back at all. They told me Kristy would never be "well," because there is no cure for bipolar. With treatment and medication, however, they had high hopes Kristy could overcome the illness and live a "normal" life.

When Kristy left the state hospital, after thirty days of in-patient care, and went to the day treatment program, she was still delusional and grandiose. During her six months in the day treatment program, Kristy worked very hard with her doctors, took an active part in her treatments, and took her medication as prescribed. I am very proud of her. I can see a tremendous improvement.

Everyday we have to keep in mind that if Kristy stops her medications, she can become manic and start the episodes all over again. That thought in itself has been sobering enough to make Kristy very aware of the need to take her medications consistently. I feel that Kristy is finally on track to managing her illness.

Despite the doctors' inability to diagnose Kristy as needing mental health assistance when she was younger, it was the diagnoses that they had given over the years, such as anxiety disorder, spastic colon, nervous stomach, and mild depression, that made me aware Kristy was covering up emotions and internal battles that she refused to share with doctors, family, or friends. In all due respect, I think the doctors who could not give a full diagnosis on Kristy gave a diagnosis as best they could with the limited information they could get from her. But everyone needs to know that bipolar by any other name is still bipolar.

Kristy has come a long way since December 20, 1999. Gone are the mood swings and delusions. The medications have her stabilized and she is getting back to a normal lifestyle. She sees her friends; they go shopping, to the movies, and to concerts. She and I go shopping and out to eat. Crowds don't bother her anymore. We laugh and joke and have a great time together. We are making plans for the future. Kristy is making plans for what she wants to do with her life, and I'm making plans for when I retire. She is volunteering at the Arts Center and has signed up for classes at the local college. She is handling life much the same as any twenty-two-year-old would.

Kristy has come a long way in her illness. A notable difference can be seen in her since the time she wrote this poem during her illness.

> A child of innocence
> in a desolate world
> telling her fears
> giving her tears
> shedding on the fright
> waiting on the light
> hurt in another's right
> I can only be hurt at night
> that's a lie
> I never feel the pain...twice the same
> always the same
> I always feel the pain.

We know that medication and doctors' visits will always play a part in Kristy's life, but we are both thankful that our story has a happy ending. I hope Kristy's story encourages people to get the help they need.

KRISTY'S STORY

THE BLACK HOLE OF
MY RACING THOUGHTS

I first noticed the highs and lows in my moods when I was about thirteen years old. I was afraid to say anything to anyone; afraid they wouldn't understand or believe that my thoughts were racing so fast inside my head that it was hard for me to keep up with them. I tried to ignore what was going on but the moods would frighten me and make me feel out of control—I couldn't even control my own thoughts. It was like I was in some black hole and couldn't find my way out.

After I turned fourteen, the mood swings got worse and closer together. Not only were my thoughts racing around inside my head, but I would have feelings of extreme excitability and then be extremely depressed. I had always been reserved and more on the shy side, but now I would have days when I would be really outgoing, as if I was on some kind of high, but I wasn't taking any drugs. Sometimes I would have anxiety attacks, where I was fearful of other people and my surroundings, or I would be really irritable for no reason.

It was getting more difficult for me to hide my moods from my family, and after a few outbursts in front of my mother, she took me to the doctor to see what was making me act the way I was.

I was afraid to tell the doctor the truth about my racing thoughts. I didn't think he would understand if I told him all the things going on inside my head. The doctor said I had mild depression and prescribed an antidepressant. I was afraid to take the medication because I was afraid it would medicate me to the point that I would not be able to hide my moods from my family and friends and that it would make me lose what little control I had over my racing thoughts. I would take the medicine for a day or two and then not take it any more.

I didn't know what was wrong with me, but I knew it was more than depression. As time went on, I had severe mood swings that would really frighten me. I didn't know how to stop them so I just drifted through them. The moods affected my concentration and I couldn't study, so I didn't do well in school or at home. I was told to straighten up, snap out of it, conform to society's rules, and pay more attention. The teachers would send notes home on my report cards: "Kristy needs to pay more attention in class; she is not working up to her full potential." I would try to do better, but instead of doing better, the notes caused me to do worse. The harder I tried to do better, the more stress it put me under. My thoughts sped up even more, which caused less concentration and more of the undesirable actions I was trying to curb so I could hide the moods from my family and the school faculty. My dad worked at the school, and I wanted him to be proud of me. I wanted from him the understanding that he gave the other students who were having problems. I wanted to work hard and make good grades like I did in elementary school. I wanted to understand myself and have other people understand me.

But I couldn't conquer the racing thoughts that were causing all the problems long enough to do any of that. No matter how hard I fought the racing thoughts, it was a battle I couldn't win. I couldn't understand the moods myself, so how could I expect others to? No one besides my mom ever said, "Kristy, we think something is wrong. We think you are trying hard but something won't let you concentrate. We think you are sick." My mom said that often and would try to get me to go see a doctor.

My friends and teachers thought my mom was overreacting to my moods when she would say something was wrong with me.

I was too afraid to admit that she might be right. The teachers thought it was a behavior problem; my friends just thought I was strange and there was nothing really wrong with me. I knew if everyone else thought that, my mom must be wrong and everyone else must be right. Their assumptions helped fuel my self-denial and allowed me to assure myself they were right.

I learned quickly that if I dressed differently and acted accordingly, people would think I was acting out and wouldn't question the actions brought on by my mood swings and my depression. This was not rational thinking, but when you are bipolar and undiagnosed, you do a lot of things that are not rational. Because I felt I was different, it made me nervous to be around other people.

After high school, I went to work in a retail store. I had to work hard to keep my moods under control. Despite my haphazard behavior, I worked hard and somehow managed to do well on the job. I was always on time and never missed work—even when I was in a manic state and staying up day and night. I still managed to drag myself to work and do a good job. Maybe part of that was because my employer and work associates believed in me. My employer always told me what a good job I was doing. This made me feel good about myself and gave me the confidence I needed to continue to do a good job.

In October of 1997, my boyfriend and I went to New Orleans on a trip. We were about fifteen miles out of New Orleans when my boyfriend fell asleep at the wheel. We hit a bridge embankment and the car flipped. I was thrown out of the car. This was the second time I had been in a car accident and thrown out of the car. The accident took off my left ear, cut up the left side of my face, and hurt my back and legs. After I got out of the hospital and started feeling better, my boyfriend and I moved to St. Louis. I had healed enough to start plastic surgery to repair my ear and the side of my face.

During this time my moods were getting worse; the highs and lows were almost unbearable. After about a year in St. Louis, we moved back to Little Rock. Things got really bad then. The cycles were more rapid than ever before, and it was hard for me to have any periods where I felt good. I was either manic or depressed all the time.

As 1999 turned into fall, I began what is known as "rapid cycling." I went from highs to lows in a very short time, with more intensity than ever. I began to think I was superhuman. I thought I didn't need to sleep or eat and felt I could do anything. I was losing a lot of weight according to my friends, but I didn't recognize it—even though I went down to eighty-six pounds. I knew my mom was worried about me and had wanted me to see a doctor, but I was still afraid to go.

The illness was becoming too much for me, and I didn't think I could go on. I began having suicidal thoughts. I called my mom around the middle of December and asked if I could stay with her. Somehow I felt I would be safe if I was with her. I was beginning to scare myself. I was either having suicidal thoughts or I was obsessed with reading the Bible. At times I thought I was Jesus. My mom came and got me and took me to her house. I don't remember much from that time up until I was in day treatment classes, because most of the time I was delusional.

I only recall bits and pieces of my stay in the hospital. I remember the doctors telling me I had an illness called bipolar. I kept saying, "Not me, this is just how I am." I remember thinking I was Jesus and that I had to write the Bible. I would copy the Bible word for word. My parents came to see me while I was in the hospital, but their visits took away time from my writing the Bible so I told them I was "divorcing" them. My mom and dad are divorced, so maybe that is where the thought came from. I remember being very adamant about them not coming. My mom came anyway because she understood it was the illness talking, not me.

During treatment, I learned that a lot of bipolar people have delusions where they think they are Jesus or God. I have thought a lot about that, and in my opinion, perhaps the reason patients feel that way is because the illness strips us of all reality, of who we really are, when we are delusional. We do and say things that seem to make perfect sense to us, but are far from being truly sensible. Since Christ is the center core of each person, that is the only thing that can't be stripped away. Perhaps we try to become that core because it is all that is left of us. The Bible tells us that Jesus says He will never leave us, and maybe that thought is the only connecting thread between the person who is delusional and his or her sanity. Even in my darkest hour, I kept trying to hang on to sanity. I'm glad my mother was able to get me help that night before I committed suicide, but if I had done it, I think God would have been like my mom. He would've known it was the illness and not me who did it.

After I spent thirty days in the hospital I was sent to the Little Rock Community Mental Health Center Day Treatment Program. Day treatment was good for me, because there were other people there that had the same illness I had. They understood what I was going through and didn't think I was different or strange. It gave me hope.

I learned these racing thoughts and weird feelings were an illness, and I could get better. I learned that other people were experiencing the same feelings that I had. I learned it was important to take my medications and follow my doctor's instructions.

One of the most important things day treatment taught me was that to be able to cope with an illness, it is important to *understand* the illness. They told me I would need to learn about bipolar so I would be able to make healthy decisions and be more in control of my moods and my life.

At first I didn't like the group sessions, because we were supposed to open ourselves up in front of others and talk to them about what was bothering us. I had always been a private person and never talked to anyone about my problems, and now to have to talk to strangers about personal things in a group—I wasn't going to do it. But then I found that talking with a group that was experiencing the same feelings that I was helped me work through those feelings and feel better about myself and more in control of my moods.

At first I wasn't going to take the medicines that my doctor prescribed, either. My peers at day treatment helped me understand the importance of taking the meds, and now that I have been on the medication I feel better about myself. I don't have anxiety attacks. I'm more comfortable around people and crowds. I no longer have the mood swings. I do not think I'm Jesus or have other delusions. I am more at peace with myself.

At day treatment I learned to watch for the symptoms of mania, which include an inflated sense of self-importance, less need for sleep, being hyper or talkative, flight of ideas or racing thoughts, becoming easily distracted, an increase in physical activity, and over-involvement in potentially harmful or risky behavior.

I also know how to recognize the symptoms of a depressive episode coming on, which may include sleeping more than usual, appetite changes, difficulty in concentrating, aches and pains with no physical cause, suicidal thoughts and/or attempts, and feeling extremely sad, worthless, or guilty. I've been through all of those feelings before, and I would recognize them if they happened again.

I know to watch for triggers that can bring on an episode of bipolar. Some triggers to look for are becoming stressed, something that makes me angry, something that would set off destructive behavior, fatigue, losing sleep, and emotional upsets. I am learning to avoid or overcome the triggers that can bring on the episodes. Sometimes triggers can't be avoided and need to be overcome with coping skills, which I also learned in treatment.

At day treatment I learned that positive coping skills include talking with others about problems and concerns, doing reality checks, taking walks, self-talk or talking to a friend, getting away from the trigger, and being able to say no to the trigger. Some negative coping skills are drinking, overeating, withdrawing, and oversleeping.

Day treatment has taught me that if I feel like I am getting out of control, I may be having a relapse. I must act immediately by calling my doctor and my support person, or if my support person sees any of the relapse signs and I won't call my doctor, then she needs to do it for me, even if I tell her not to. The warning signs of relapse to look for are overeating, not getting enough sleep, not taking medicine, attempting or talking suicide, turning to alcohol or drugs, and bizarre behavior. My mom is my support person, and she helps me do reality checks on a regular basis, and I know if she sees any signs of relapse, she will call the doctor immediately, whether I like it or not. That is what she is supposed to do.

Day treatment has also taught me that I need to think positive and believe in myself. To do that I need to realize that I am a special person and have a right to all my feelings. I can trust myself even when I fail. I have a right to be loved. I am a kind and loving person. I am playful and fun to be around. I have good qualities to offer myself and others. I have the right to be admired and appreciated just for being me. I deserve good things to come my way. It's okay to make a mistake. I'm not perfect but I still have many talents. Everyone needs to apply all of the above to themselves to have good self-esteem and feel good about themselves. It is important to read motivational and inspirational books, talk with positive people, and do things you enjoy that are healthy for you. Eat healthy, nutritional meals and exercise.

In our classes we learned that we had to move beyond the illness by moving back into the mainstream of life: visiting friends, going places, going to classes, and going back to work, if possible. Before I went into the hospital, work was the one thing that gave me confidence in myself and made me feel independent and in control of my life. I will be glad when I am stable enough to return to work, but meanwhile, since I have finished my day treatment classes, a transition that is working well for me is doing some volunteer work on a part-time basis. One day soon I will be stronger and able to return to work on a full-time basis.

If you are experiencing some of the same thoughts and feelings that I went through, I want to encourage you to see a doctor and tell the doctor *everything*. He or she can't fully diagnose you unless you disclose exactly what is going on. Take your medications, follow your doctor's instructions, and if at all possible, participate in a day treatment program so you can learn more about your illness, learn coping skills, and overcome your feelings of hopelessness. I spent six months in day treatment classes, and they have really helped me. I still keep the folder I got at day treatment classes with all the handouts on how to cope with bipolar and make healthy decisions. I still keep a journal to record my moods. I take my medications, keep my doctor's appointments, and stay in contact with my support group and case worker. I listen to and act on the things my mother points out in our reality checks. My mother encourages me to be independent, to go places, do things on my own, and make plans for my future. I am becoming more in control of my thoughts and my actions. I know there is no cure for bipolar, that I will always have to see my doctor, and stay on my medications, but by doing that I can manage the symptoms and lead a life that is fulfilling and successful. At last I feel I have found a way out of the black hole of my racing thoughts. I want everyone to have the chance that I have had to get more in control of their moods and to be able to feel more at peace with themselves.

BIPOLAR:
WHAT IS IT?

Bipolar disorder is a medical condition that is thought to be caused by a chemical imbalance in the brain. The illness can be brought on by stress, although not much else is known about what causes its onset. It is characterized by mood swings, which can go from incredible highs to depressing lows. Thus the name *bipolar*, meaning more than one mood.*

There are several phases to bipolar: the manic stage, the depression stage, mixed mania, and rapid cycling. You may experience one or all of the phases followed by periods of relatively normal behavior. The mood swings can be very dramatic and difficult for you and your family to manage. Therefore it is very important for you and your family to see that you receive professional help.

MANIC BEHAVIOR

When you are in the manic stage of bipolar, you may feel unusually high, as if you are in total control of the world. You may feel superhuman, as if you can do anything. You may take irrational risks and do things that you would not do if you were not experiencing this manic episode. Your speech may become

* *Many thanks to Carol Peckham and Nidus Information Services for the information in the following chapter. Please see "Bipolar Disorder, a Well-Connected Report," by Harvey B. Simon, Editor-in-Chief, Nidus Information Services, Inc., © 2000 for more details, or visit www.well-connected.com.*

rapid, and you may have racing thoughts, thoughts racing through your mind so fast that it is difficult for you to concentrate on or remember things. You may rhyme your words, which is a symptom called "clanging" and is not unusual for a patient in the manic state of bipolar.

You probably will not realize that any of these symptoms are out of the ordinary, because you believe that this is just your normal way of doing things. Those around you, though, will notice the difference.

You may become irritable with others because they don't understand your actions or are unable to keep up with your racing thoughts and your rapid speech. When you are in the manic stage you may have additional energy. Your racing thoughts may have your body "revved up" and feeling superhuman. You may not feel the need for food or rest.

The illness is classified as either bipolar I or bipolar II. People who have bipolar I may experience depressive and manic episodes or just manic episodes. People with bipolar II suffer primarily from depressive episodes with occasional bouts of hypomania, but they do not experience full-blown manic episodes. In most cases of bipolar disorder, the depressive episodes outnumber the manic episodes, and the cycles of mania and depression are not regular or predictable. In a subtype of the illness known as "rapid cycling," the manic and depressive stages alternate at least four times a year, and in severe cases can progress to several cycles a day.

Bipolar disorder has been a difficult illness to diagnose for years, and only in the last forty years have doctors begun to understand the disorder and to develop successful treatments. Scientists are still trying to come up with ways to effectively diagnose the disorder. In one study of people with bipolar disorder, MRI scans of the brain have revealed structural abnormalities in the hippocampus. The left side of the hippocampus was significantly larger than the right. The pathways of the neurotransmitter dopamine also appear to be important. (A neurotransmitter acts as a chemical messenger between nerve cells.) Dopamine has been a target of scientific investigation since researchers first observed that certain drugs that reduce the action of dopamine in the brain also reduce psychotic symptoms. Currently researchers are seeking ways to discover factors in the blood that might help diagnose bipolar disorder and determine the effectiveness of its treatment. There is no evidence yet that can be readily used for diagnostic purposes.

Bipolar disorder can be severe and long term, or it can be mild with infrequent episodes. A typical bipolar patient averages eight to ten manic or depressive episodes over a lifetime, but some sufferers experience much more severe symptoms or rapid cycles. An estimated fifteen to twenty percent of patients who suffer from bipolar and who do not receive medical attention commit suicide; in spite of this alarming death rate, only one third of bipolar sufferers receive treatment. Even with therapy, one or more relapses occur in most patients.

Bipolar patients need an enormous amount of support to help avoid the risky behavior common in manic episodes and to fight against the low self-esteem and guilt experienced during the depressed phases. During all stages of the illness, patients need to be reminded that the mood disturbances will pass, and that the disorder's severity can be diminished by treatment.

Despite the obvious need for professional help, access to medical therapies is not always available for patients with bipolar disorder. In one major survey, thirteen percent of patients had no insurance and fifteen percent were unable to afford medical treatment.

The symptoms of depression experienced in bipolar disorder are almost identical to those of major clinical depression. A manic episode usually comes on suddenly, and it often but not always follows a period of severe depression. Symptoms of a manic episode include rapid speech, disconnected thoughts, grandiose ideas, hallucinations, and extreme irritability. Irritability is most often the first noticeable change in behavior at the onset of a manic phase. The patient often requires little sleep; some experts suggest that sleep loss may actually trigger or intensify mania. Close to sixty percent of all manic patients experience feelings of omnipotence, sometimes believing that they are godlike or have celebrity status. Some patients experience a marked increase in strength in the manic stages.

Bipolar is a widespread illness. Between one and two million Americans are thought to suffer from bipolar disorder. Estimates of the lifetime risk for the disorder run between one and one and a half percent.

Bipolar disorder affects both sexes equally, but women are almost three times more likely than men to experience rapid cycling. However, rapid cycling occurs in between ten and fifteen percent of all bipolar patients.

Manic phases usually begin in adolescence or young adulthood, with average age of onset being eighteen. Bipolar disorder, however, has been known to appear for the first time in people over forty years of age.

The time of year appears to play a role in increasing the risk for episodes. In one study, men appeared to have more episodes during the spring and women were at higher risk during the spring and fall. The rate of bipolar disorder is estimated to be ten to twenty times higher among people in the creative arts than in the general population. People who are alcoholic may also be at higher risk for bipolar disorder.

DEPRESSION

The depression part of bipolar disorder can take sufferers from regular depression to some of the lowest "lows" that it is possible to experience. Symptoms of depression include paranoia, a desire to sleep all the time, headaches, stomachaches, and backaches that can't be found by a physician and do not respond to treatment, irritability, and periods of extreme sadness.

Some people have suicidal thoughts, and without professional help, they may act on those thoughts. It is of extreme importance to get medical help immediately if you experience any feelings that may cause you to want to harm yourself or others.

Depression can be a devastating experience. When it is at its peak, a dark cloud seems to pervade one's being. The person afflicted may try valiantly to check its progress and yet it seems to advance with relentless strength. It may start in the head as a dark presence, then moves to fill the whole body. When it has taken over completely, life hardly seems worth living.

Depression is more than just "the blues." Depression is not a personal weakness. Symptoms of depression affect thoughts, feelings, body, and behaviors. Without treatment the symptoms can last for months, years, or a lifetime.

Some depressive episodes occur suddenly for no apparent reason. Some are triggered by a stressful experience. Some people's symptoms are so severe that they are unable to function as usual. Others have ongoing, chronic symptoms that do not interfere with functioning, but keep the person from feeling really well. Nearly two-thirds of depressed people do not get appropriate treatment because their symptoms are so disabling they cannot reach out for help, or they are misdiagnosed and wrongly treated. With proper treatment, eighty percent of people with serious depression—even those with the most severe forms—can improve significantly. Symptoms can be relieved usually in a matter of weeks.

Evaluation and treatment can be received from physicians, mental health specialists, community mental health centers, hospital departments of psychiatry or outpatient psychiatric clinics, university- or medical school-affiliated programs, state hospital outpatient clinics, or private clinics and facilities. In addition to treatment, joining a support group may be helpful.

The very nature of depressive illnesses can interfere with a person's ability or wish to get help. Depression saps energy and self-esteem and makes a person feel tired, worthless, helpless, and hopeless. Therefore seriously depressed people need encouragement from family and friends to seek treatment to ease their pain. Some people may need even more help, becoming so depressed they must be taken for treatment. Don't ignore suicidal thoughts, words, or acts. Seek professional help immediately.

Depression is the result of a chemical imbalance in the brain. Antidepressants, if taken in the right dosage over a finite period of time, allow the brain to be healed of this imbalance. Future research will be done on depression. Its insidious cause eventually may be recognized. Perhaps someday it will be preventable.

Until this breakthrough occurs, the route of medication brings hope. Medication takes time to work, however, and the depression can be a lingering condition.

MIXED MANIA

You may experience symptoms of both the manic phase and the depressive phase at the same time. This is called "mixed mania." You may feel excited, have increased energy, and then go through periods of feeling sad and hopeless. These symptoms may be followed by long or short periods of feeling normal.

RAPID CYCLING

Rapid cycling occurs less frequently than the other phases of bipolar. It occurs when a patient alternates often between mania and depression. As a patient, you may feel "high" or elated and then within a short while be very depressed. While in this stage you may suffer from some psychotic symptoms, such as believing you have special powers or that you may be God or someone else. You may experience paranoia.

Not all patients with bipolar may have all the different symptoms or have them to the same degree of intensity. It is important to talk with your doctor about any unusual feelings.

Bipolar is a persistent medical condition, just as diabetes, high blood pressure, cancer, and heart disease are persistent medical conditions. It is important to recognize and understand that bipolar disorder is not the result of some flaw in your character or something that you did, and your struggle with the illness is not a sign of personal weakness or lack of willpower on your part.

Bipolar is nothing to be ashamed of, and you should continue to lead your life as normally as possible while following your doctor's orders and staying on your medication.

It is important for you to understand that bipolar disorder can affect anyone, regardless of race, sex, education, occupation, or income.

Even though bipolar can run in families, genetics does not always explain who gets it and who doesn't. Even though no one knows for sure what causes bipolar, scientists believe the symptoms may be activated by a chemical imbalance in the brain.

Most cases of bipolar disorder can be controlled by staying under the care of a doctor and taking medication exactly as prescribed. Without treatment, the illness can be so dramatic that it may impair your ability to function normally at work, school, or in relationships. You can come to the point where you are delusional and may have to spend time in a hospital.

Don't you think it would be easier to talk with your doctor and take your medication than to go through the delusions and spend time in the hospital? Kristy and I have been there, and we can tell you firsthand that it is a lot better to follow the doctors' orders and take the prescribed medication.

Following is a poem that Kristy wrote when she was in a delusional state:

The placid child we once knew
is now plagued with anguish
a veil of violence adorns her face
when anguish sets in
it is now time to dissemble
metamorphosis takes place
the palpitation produces vertigo
the phantom of the shrew appears now distempered
the complete destruction of all things in view
enraged now for all its worth
all that is left is shattered glass
the shattered hearts, the sea of tears
all things dyed with blood
my "eau de vie" is now dry
slip back through the port holes
to get back to serenity for eternity
no time to replenish the mind, body and soul

that have all been drained, time to focus
strive to mend all things broken
clarity for eternity
a replenished "eau de vie"

Can you imagine the torment inside oneself that would produce a poem of such emotion?

WHAT CAN BE DONE ABOUT IT?

Even though there is no cure for bipolar disorder, most patients find that their symptoms can be managed by medications, psychotherapy, and support systems. In some cases there may be a need for hospitalization or day treatment programs, at least for a period of time.*

After you have been diagnosed and your doctor has decided on a plan of action for you—whether it be hospitalization, day treatment, or scheduled appointments—your doctor will prescribe medication to help you manage your symptoms.

One of the main medications that helped control the symptoms of bipolar for my daughter, Kristy, was Zyprexa. Zyprexa is a mood-stabilizer that helps with the manic phase of bipolar disorder. It is believed that Zyprexa may work by correcting the elements of the chemical imbalance that causes the symptoms of bipolar disorder. Zyprexa may not be for everyone, but it has worked wonders for my daughter, helping to stabilize her moods and enabling her to return to normal activities in a more normal lifestyle.

Zyprexa, along with the other medications that Kristy's doctor has prescribed, is helping her move beyond the illness and lead a normal life.

* Many thanks to Carol Peckham and Nidus Information Services for the information in the following chapter. Please see "Bipolar Disorder, a Well-Connected Report," by Harvey B. Simon, Editor-in-Chief, Nidus Information Services, Inc., © 2000 for more details, or visit www.well-connected.com.

It is important to always take the medications that your doctor prescribes exactly as you are told. Do not stop taking the medicines until your doctor tells you to and only take the medications that your doctor prescribes.

Everyone's illness is different, so your doctor may prescribe different medications according to your symptoms.

If your doctor prescribes hospitalization, it may be in a private hospital or a state hospital. It is an emotional time for both the patient and the family when hospitalization is required. Almost every city has a hospital for patients suffering with bipolar or other emotional disorders. Most of these are staffed with doctors and nurses and caregivers to help the patient regain control of his or her emotions and go home as soon as possible.

State hospitals are not the horror stories you often read about or see on TV. Kristy spent thirty days in the Arkansas state hospital and received wonderful care. She had doctors and staff who were very professional, yet caring and sensitive. When Kristy was admitted, she was delusional and not eating or sleeping. They were able to diagnose her illness, prescribe medications to help lessen the delusions, help her start eating and sleeping, and get her back on the road to managing her illness.

Day treatment programs are essentially just that. The patient attends classes on a daily basis at a mental health center, where he or she attends group sessions with others suffering from bipolar disorder, as well as individual sessions with a doctor. Patients learn about their illness, how to help manage it, and the importance of staying on their medication.

The length of time that you will need to remain in the day treatment program will be decided by you and your doctor. Because of the level of dysfunction Kristy was at when she entered the treatment program, she was asked to stay for six months, to give her and the doctors time to level out her moods, teach her about the illness, and stabilize her on medications.

Kristy attended classes from 9 A.M. to 2:30 P.M. Monday through Friday. After her first day, she came in and announced, "I'm not going back, I don't need those classes!" I convinced her to try it one more day. We went through the same scenario on a daily basis for at least two weeks. If it wasn't the classes she didn't need, it was the medication. She would say, "I'm not taking this stuff, it's not doing me any good!"

Somewhere between two and three weeks into the day treatment program, she adjusted to the idea of going to class and taking her medications. Her delusions finally stopped, and she was able to focus and understand that she *did* have an illness and that she *did* need treatment. (Counting her thirty days in the state hospital, she had already been under treatment for forty-five to fifty days.)

Somewhere around the third month, she began to share with me some of the things she was learning about her illness. By the end of the fifth month, she was more open about her illness and was taking an active role in her treatments. By the end of the sixth month, when she was completing her classes, Kristy agreed to do a documentary video about her illness to be used as an educational video for Eli Lilly and Company, the makers of Zyprexa. The video is available to doctors and other groups across the United States to help others with bipolar. It may also be viewed on the Internet at www.zyprexa.com.

To say that Kristy has come a long way would be an understatement. She entered the state hospital delusional, not knowing who she was, started day treatment classes still delusional and very grandiose, and after six months of day treatments is now making plans to go back to school, go back to work, and move on with her life.

Once you have completed your hospital stay and your day treatments, your doctor will probably see you once every two weeks or once a month, depending on what your doctor thinks is best for you. The doctor will prescribe medications for you to take. It is very important to take your medication exactly as your doctor prescribes. Follow any instructions he or she may give you on activities and diet and keep all of your doctors' appointments. By doing this you are taking an active part in your treatment and helping to manage your illness.

Today there is a lot that can be done about bipolar or manic depressive disorder. Science is making giant strides in medications and treatments for patients.

Patients should understand that even with aggressive therapy, relapse of either mania or depression occurs in almost three quarters of patients. Even in those who do not relapse, depression is common. The preferred class of drugs used for bipolar disorder are mood-stabilizers, but many other types also may be required to manage specific conditions, such as depressive episodes and rapid cycling.

Although bipolar disorder is the result of chemical imbalances in the brain, psychological support is a key feature of treatment for all phases of the problem. Psychiatrists or trained psychological professionals monitor the patient's ongoing status and intervene as early as possible in manic and depressive episodes in order to reduce the severity of the attack. Psychotherapists and other mental health professionals can also educate patients about the disorder and its treatment and can help them make social and psychological adaptations, and to comply with drug regimens. Just as importantly, therapists and counselors must help patients cope with feelings of guilt and remorse in response to their actions during mania and with feelings of imperfection and despair when they acknowledge their illness. These feelings would be difficult enough in a healthy individual, but the accompanying depression, which places the patient in danger of suicide, often compounds them. Therapy focused on improving self-esteem, rebuilding social support, and making sure the patient complies with other medical therapies is therefore essential.

It is very important for psychotherapists who treat patients with bipolar disorder to meet with family, partners, or close friends to help strengthen the social and emotional supports that are so necessary for patients with bipolar disorder. Relatives of bipolar patients must be encouraged to maintain support because there is a high risk of suicide if support evaporates.

Family and friends of people with bipolar disorder can offer support by listening attentively and by being empathetic. The patient should not be made to feel guilty; bipolar disorder results from a chemical imbalance in the brain—it is not his or her fault. Family members of bipolar patients must be strong and forceful in getting the patient to comply with treatment and keeping his or her appointments. Family members should have on hand at all times a hotline number or the number of a psychiatrist authorized to commit the patient if they have a relapse. Relapse occurs in most patients after treatment of acute attacks, and patients who are at high risk for recurring episodes should consider lifelong maintenance therapy.

HOW BIPOLAR AFFECTS YOUR LIFE AND YOUR LOVED ONES

Bipolar disorder can alter your life in several ways. Without treatment, you may not be able to function properly, hold a job, attend school, or take part in normal everyday life with your family and friends.

Without treatment, bipolar can cause you to become delusional and make you think you are superhuman. During these times of delusions, you may say or do things you would not otherwise do. You may think you are Jesus Christ, a demon, or some other person or creature that your manic mind has created.

Because of intense emotions during mania or depression, you may become irritable and yell at people or not communicate with anyone, which could cause you to lose your job if you are working. With treatment and medication, however, most people with bipolar are able to go back to their job and/or school and lead a normal lifestyle.

Because most of the public is not educated about mental illnesses, you may have to deal with people's negative attitudes when they find out you have bipolar. Mental illness, though unfairly, still has a stigma attached to it. As devastating as it is to cope with the illness, sometimes sufferers must endure the misconceptions of the public as well.

The only way to manage the stigma is to face it head-on. The more you and/or your family try to cover up the fact that you have bipolar, the harder it will be for you to come to terms with the illness, and the longer it will take for you to get well.

With time and education, I hope that the general public will come to realize that mental illness is just like heart disease, cancer, diabetes, or any other illness. Bipolar disorder may not have a cure, but it can normally be controlled with medication and by following doctors' orders.

Bipolar disorder is difficult for family members to understand and deal with, yet family support during the illness is one of the main things that helps the patient get back on track. The roller coaster of emotions is hard to understand for the patient as well as for the family members. It is sometimes difficult for the family to deal with the depression and the mania, and very difficult for the family to deal with some of the problems brought on by a full-blown mania episode like I went through with Kristy.

Parents, especially, find it hard to cope when the child has not yet been diagnosed as bipolar. In adolescence, bipolar can be mistaken for delinquent behavior. The mania episodes of being aggressive, grandiose, rapid, or having slurred speech can sometimes be mistaken for drug or alcohol use or just hatefulness or rebellion, all actions that parents find difficult to deal with.

When the adolescent is depressed and doesn't want to go places or to be around other people, and just wants to sleep all the time, parents may view this as laziness and rudeness, not understanding that this behavior is caused by depression.

Any outbursts of anger or voiced concerns by the parents magnify the illness to the patient, and just at a time when they are needed the most, the parents can become fed up with the situation and ask the adolescent to leave the house, not knowing that their child is battling an illness.

One parent may feel there is more to the situation than meets the eye. Sides are picked and then there is a rift in the family, sometimes leading to divorce, siblings fighting each other, or members leaving the house. It is an emotional time for all family members until the patient has been diagnosed and leveled out with medication and treatment.

As the patient levels out, the family may then be at "overload" from being the caregivers. Stress begins to build up in the family. Usually one family member becomes the support system for the patient, and at times that person may feel overwhelmed with all the "normal" duties piled on the additional duty of being the support person. The caregiver may become tired and discouraged. It is at this time that other family members should step in and help with the support system, so the main caregiver doesn't burn out.

Frequently, family members will blame themselves or each other for the patient being bipolar. At times, family members may feel disappointed that the patient may not get to continue with dreams the patient has—or the dreams that the family has for the patient.

There are support groups for families that can help them learn to handle situations as they arise. If you take part in the support groups, you can learn how to manage all the feelings that come up before things get to a crisis situation. NAMI (the National Association of Mental Illness) has an educational support program called Family to Family that can really help.

Friends sometimes do not understand the illness or why patients and caregivers act the way they do, therefore you may lose some of the people you thought were friends. They may be embarrassed or uncomfortable talking about the illness, afraid that they will say or do the wrong thing.

It usually takes away some of the awkwardness if you are comfortable enough to explain bipolar to your friends, and let them know that as long as you take your medication and continue to see your doctor, you can lead your life much the same as you did before the illness. Real friends will stick by you, regardless of good times or bad times. If you have to make new friends, then so be it. You are a worthwhile person, and we all have to make new starts and adjustments as we go through life. You can win the daily battle by following your treatment plan and taking your medication while we are waiting on science to win the war by coming up with the cure for bipolar and/or new and better medications and treatments to manage the symptoms.

In the following poem that Kristy wrote during her illness, she relates the effects the illness was having on her at the time:

> Perfidy, atrociousity, animosity
> Perdition catches one's attention
> Quick to spin in circles,
> When not knowing life's cycles
> What would you think
> If it happened to you?
> The world just clicked,
> A revelation fell into your hands,
> Left to sort through it all,
> Not knowing whether to sink or stall.
> Helpless not hopeless,
> What does it bring?
> Face fate with faith in everything
> If you are in sin
> Travail will prevail
> No secrecy, no need to lie
> Justice, just is, justified.

In the poem she talks about not knowing life's cycles. How close she was to understanding that bipolar has its own cycles! Then the pointed question, "What would you think if it happened to you?" In the poem, she talks of spinning in circles: she would do just that, little "ballerina-like dances" around the room. Not only were her thoughts spinning in circles, but her movements were also. Even in her delusions and poem writing, Kristy was trying to make sense of the illness.

MOVING BEYOND THE ILLNESS

Once you have been diagnosed as bipolar, your hospitalization or day treatment classes are over, your medications have leveled out your moods, and you begin to feel better, it is time to move beyond the illness.

Moving beyond the illness does not mean to stop taking your medication or to stop seeing your doctor. It means that because you are feeling better and are more stable, you may want to go back to work or back to school, or follow a routine much the same as you did before your illness began.

If you are not ready for full-time work or classes, you may want to start with part-time work or classes or do some volunteer work. It is essential to follow as normal a routine as possible.

Occasionally you may gain weight while on the medications. This is usually because the medications make you crave carbohydrates, and you may not be as active as you were before the illness. Ask your doctor before changing your diet, but if you are gaining weight, your doctor may suggest a low-carbohydrate diet and exercise to help you lose some of the extra pounds and maintain a weight that you and your doctor have decided is right for you.

You are not alone in the illness of bipolar. A lot of famous people have fought the battle of bipolar: Bach, Michaelangelo, Patty Duke, Robin Williams, and Kay Redfield Jamison, to name a few, as well as many people like yourself. With medication and by taking an active part in your treatments, you can move back into the normal activities you always enjoyed.

Another important part of mental and physical health is learning to feel good about yourself—having a good self-image.

We never see ourselves as others see us. We see ourselves as our mind has told us we are. Therefore, if our mind has told us we are worthless, plain looking, bad, and non-communicative, then that is how we see ourselves. Others may see there is a better side to us—see that we are bright, talented, and worthwhile—but for us to see that same thing we have to build a better self-image.

We all deserve to feel good about ourselves and to have a healthy self-image. First, let's take a look at how we can think our way to a better self-image.

We all talk to ourselves. Some people call it thinking; some people call it self talk. As our thoughts are swirling around inside our heads, we are talking to ourselves. I have been told that we talk to ourselves approximately seventy percent of the time in any given day.

The average person has a multitude of negative messages circulating in his mind at any given moment. It is said that the average person speaks aloud at the rate of 150 to 250 words per minute. The average self talk or thinking occurs at the rate of over eight hundred words per minute, especially if you are embarrassed or mad. (Reprinted from *Secrets of Power Presentations* by Micki Holliday, Franklin Lakes, NJ: Career Press.)

Think back to a time when you did something that embarrassed you. Remember how fast your thoughts told you what an idiot you were, or reprimanded you for not doing what was right instead of doing the embarrassing thing. Or perhaps someone said things to you or about you that made you feel bad about yourself or feel fearful that you would never be able to do or say the right things. These are called negative thoughts.

Yet you can turn the negative messages into positive affirmations. Positive self talk reverses fear by overriding it. Positive thinking instills confidence, and confidence allows actions that you can take to overcome fear.

Negative self talk magnifies fears, promotes self doubt, and instills "I can't" thinking. Positive self talk focuses on possibilities, positive outcomes, and "can do" thinking. Effective self talk can help put things into perspective.

Take into consideration that the above information is based on normal, healthy people. Can you imagine the speed of the thoughts going through the mind of someone with bipolar disorder in a state of mania? We know their speech speeds up as they go into mania, and we know that racing thoughts is part of the bipolar illness.

If we take what we know about the patterns of regular speech and thoughts together with what we know about the pattern of speech and thoughts in people with bipolar disorder, we can use that as a foundation to build good thoughts and a good self-image. Then we are on the road to feeling good about ourselves!

We can learn to build a better self-image. It *will* take some practice. I hope you will take the time to gain a better understanding of how to build confidence in yourself. You deserve to be appreciated and recognized for the things you do.

To *stay* "beyond the illness," you need to stay on your medications and take them exactly as your doctor prescribes, keep all your doctors' appointments, eat right and get enough rest, exercise, stay active in work and social affairs, and begin building a good self-image. Learn to recognize the triggers that can bring on an episode of mania or depression and avoid or defuse them. Have a support person help you do reality checks on a regular basis.

Moving beyond the illness means getting in control of bipolar disorder and not letting it control you. You will know you have successfully moved beyond the illness when you are not focusing as much on your illness, and you are focusing more on your plans for the future.

WHAT I LEARNED AT NAMI

The crisis has settled down some. Your family member is better, not *good* maybe, but better. You are still reeling from the effects this trauma has had on you. You want to learn more about the illness and how to care for your loved one, now that he or she is home from the hospital or day treatment. Will life ever be the same? Will things ever get back to normal?

I was fortunate to find the answers to these questions and others that were just as important at NAMI Family to Family educational classes. Not only did I get answers, but I was around people who were going through the same or similar situations that I had been through. Some may be farther along in their journey and some may behind you in theirs, but wherever you are is where you start. The educational classes help you understand the illness, your role, and where to get the help you need.

NAMI (the National Association of Mental Illness) is a nationwide organization with many programs to help support families with mental illness. One of their programs is the Family to Family educational class. It is a twelve-week course designed to help family members understand mental illness. Even though NAMI is a national organization, it is broken down into state affiliates and then into areas within each state. I would encourage you to find a NAMI chapter to help you get more in control of your life and to understand your loved one's illness better.

Dealing with mental illness can be overwhelming and frightening. Because so much is going on you can begin to lose your self-confidence about how to care for your loved one. I didn't understand my daughter's illness; neither did my family and friends. No one wanted to talk about it. I felt isolated and alone. My daughter's doctor told me about NAMI, so I decided to check it out.

At the NAMI educational classes, I learned that I wasn't alone. I learned that one out of every five families have to deal with some form of mental illness. I was with other people who were going through the same or similar situations. We were all looking for coping skills to help us and our loved one through the journey we are on. We learned what to look for in ourselves and our family members that would move us forward and what was holding us back or making things worse. Through the classes, we learned how to cope and how to communicate effectively. We learned that, as the caregiver, we had to take time to care for ourselves and that we were not to blame for our loved one's illness. We learned how to get through crises and conflicts. We learned that the public at large and families as a whole have different perspectives of mental illness. Each individual has different stages of acceptance and different coping styles. We learned to turn negative emotional build-up into positive results by advocating for the rights of the mentally ill.

NAMI classes stress the importance of pulling together as a family and as a group to support our family member and all others who have any form of mental illness.

At one of the weekly meetings I was having a particularly hard time emotionally. I was under stress at work. I wasn't feeling well physically. I was concerned about Kristy. Since I'm a single parent, I felt overwhelmed trying to deal with everything at one time by myself and was also angry at myself for not being strong enough to make everything turn out okay.

During the meeting I broke into tears. I couldn't stop crying. I was totally embarrassed. Of all the members there I probably had the least to worry about, but for some reason, I had reached my breaking point. I was surprised to find everyone trying to console me and encourage me. No one thought I was weak just because I cried. They understood. Later that evening, after I had gotten home—and also the following day—several members of the class called to check on me and encourage me. I will never forget their kindness and compassion. With their thoughtfulness, I gave myself permission to accept that I was still an okay person when I cried or if I was scared and overwhelmed. Within a few days, I had sorted through the circumstances and come up with a workable solution that got me back on track, feeling in control of the situation, and feeling good about myself.

In closing, I hope this book has been a help to you and your family or someone you care about. There is help out there, as well as people who care about you. I care about *you*. That is why I wrote this book, hoping to help you through some of the struggles you are going through. Remember you are not alone. There is help! I would strongly encourage each of you to seek out and join a NAMI Family to Family educational class.

Each state has a NAMI affiliate office broken down into local offices throughout the state. Ask your doctor or look in the phone book for the nearest NAMI office and tell them you want to sign up for the classes. You will be glad you did.

Kristy and I wish for you peace, understanding, and encouragement.

We wish for you peace of mind, knowing you have done all you can to get help for yourself or your loved one. We wish for you peace in your heart and in your life.

We wish for you understanding that you have done all you can. Don't blame yourself or feel guilty for all the things you won't be able to do.

We wish for you encouragement. We want to encourage you to realize that you are not alone, and that with each new day comes the promise of better treatments, better medication, and better understanding by the public about mental illness.

If this book has been helpful to you, pass it on or recommend it to others.

Following is a poem I wrote for Kristy when she first came home from the hospital in January of 2000. She was glad to be home, yet fearful that the illness would overtake her again. I wrote the poem to let her know I would always be there to support her. Each night for several weeks after she first got home, she would ask me to read the poem to her before she went to sleep, so she would know that the illness wouldn't get her again. As she got better, we read the poem less and less, and now I don't even remember how or when we stopped reading it. I found it the other day in the drawer of the nightstand that sits beside my bed and decided it would be fitting to put in this book. I added the last verse just for that use.

It's a journey you've not chosen,
destination not known
but no matter where it takes you
I won't let you walk alone

No matter where the highs and lows
may take you to
I'll hold your hand, and take a stand
and be right there with you

Don't ever panic,
and think you can't make it through
those thoughts are just the illness
and really are not true

When the deepest of depressions
comes swirling in
I won't let you sink
I'll teach you how to swim!

When the mania peaks out
at an all-time high
I'll keep you grounded
until it passes by

When we see the delusions
come sneaking in like thieves

I won't let them steal your mind
and confuse all your beliefs

When you've had more than you can take
and you're thinking suicide
you're riding waves of destruction
that are welling up inside
I'll control the demon
and I'll turn back the tide

It's a journey you've not chosen
with pitfalls and dangerous ground
but bipolar is just an illness
that we will turn around

So take my hand and walk with me
and trust my every move
we'll ride out the journey
and I'll help you make it through!

Though it's a journey you've not chosen
our destination we have found
with medication and treatments
we have gotten to solid ground

As we move beyond the illness
lest we dare forget
Let's use our story to help those
we haven't met

And with our encouragement
help them find their way
and stand beside them
till we hear them say:

It was a journey not chosen
but *our* destination we have found

bipolar was just an illness
that we turned around

Then we will add them to our group
and still we won't forget
that it will always be our duty
to help those we haven't met.

Remember you are not alone in your illness. There are doctors, support groups, and people like Kristy and myself who want to help you get the medication and treatment you need to get better.

EDUCATIONAL MATERIALS

MENTAL ILLNESS FACT SHEET

What is mental illness?

Mental illnesses are both mental *and* physical disorders. They can severely disturb a person's ability to think, feel, and relate to other people and his or her environment. They are treatable and diagnosable, just like cancer and diabetes. People with serious mental illnesses need treatment. It is not something they can control by willpower or changing their lifestyle.

What are some of the more disabling mental illnesses? How common are they?

Schizophrenia affects nearly two million American adults each year. It is a brain disease that may cause its victims to suffer from hallucinations and an inability to distinguish real from imaginary. The cause is unknown but believed to be biological, perhaps genetic.

Depressive disorders include the two most serious disorders, major depression and manic depression. They are also the most common form of mental illness: within any given one-year period, about fifteen million Americans, or 6.3% of the population, suffers from one of these disorders. They can range widely in severity and are treated in numerous ways.

Approximately one in four Americans will suffer from a mental illness during his or her lifetime.

Mental illness is more common than cancer, diabetes, heart disease, or arthritis.

How many children and adolescents have mental or behavioral disorders?

Conduct disorder, such as Attention Deficit Hyperactivity Disorder (ADHD), is the most frequently diagnosed disorder in children and adolescents under the age of eighteen. ADHD affects three to five percent of the nation's youth under thirteen.

A conservative estimate is that seven and a half million of the country's sixty-three million children under age eighteen have mental, behavioral, or developmental disorders. Only about a fifth of those who need mental health treatment receive it.

How are persons with mental illness stigmatized?

People who suffer from mental illness are no more likely to commit an act of violence than the general population, despite the common stereotype of the mentally ill as violent and irrational. In fact, those who suffer from mental illness are more likely to be isolated, passive, and withdrawn—and therefore more likely to be victims of violence.

Disparaging labels such as "psycho" and "crazy" or "loonybin" and "insane asylum" only allow negative stereotypes to persist in society.

Victims of mental illness often find themselves discriminated against in the community by being denied housing, employment, and insurance coverage.

What are some other general facts about mental illness?

At least eighty percent of children in the juvenile justice system are identified as needing mental health treatment.

As many as twelve percent of the American population have a phobia.

Almost one-third of U.S. jails incarcerate people with severe mental illnesses who have no charges against them—people waiting for a psychiatric evaluation or admittance to a psychiatric hospital. An estimated 159,000 people currently incarcerated have some sort of severe mental illness; most are there for crimes they committed while not being treated.

Additionally, one half to one third of the homeless population has a serious mental illness. Many cannot take adequate care of themselves and remain homeless for months or years.

Roughly fifty to sixty percent of people with a serious mental illness also have a drug or alcohol problem, a condition called dual diagnosis.

The majority of people who commit or attempt suicide have a diagnosable mental or substance abuse disorder. The suicide rate for people who have a serious mental illness is ten percent.

Is there hope for persons suffering from mental illness? How can I help?

Absolutely! Scientists continue to make strides in understanding the nature and causes of mental illnesses, and they continue to work on developing treatments for them. Today, early detection and better treatments allow many sufferers to live independent, productive lives. While there are many people who do not recover and cannot live on their own, most people with mental illness are able to lead lives indistinguishable from the general population.

For schizophrenia, the treatment success rate is sixty percent; for major depression, sixty-five percent; and for bipolar disorder, eighty percent. In comparison, the success rate for treatments of heart disease ranges from only forty to sixty percent.

Friends, family, and the community can provide a much-needed part in the recovery process. Education about mental illness can go a long way to helping someone you know, as well as provision of support and understanding. Similarly, encouraging someone you suspect of suffering from a mental illness to seek help—whether from a family doctor, local community mental health center, licensed social worker, psychologist, or psychiatrist—can be a very important step in that person's recovery.

RESOURCES FOR HELP AND INFORMATION

Any of the organizations below can provide you with information or pamphlets. While only the national offices are listed here, many can refer you to the state or regional affiliate nearest you, and all of them can send you information. Remember, it's not a disgrace to have mental illness, and the more you know the more you can help.

The National Foundation For Depressive Illnesses
P.O. Box 2257
New York City, NY 10116
212-268-4260

National Depressive and Manic Depressive Association
730 North Franklin, Suite 501
Chicago, IL 60610-7204
800-826-3632
Fax: 312-642-0049

National Mental Health Association
1021 Prince Street
Alexandria, VA 22314
800-969-6642

National Association of Mental Illness (NAMI)
Colonial Place Three
2107 Wilson Blvd, 3rd Floor, Suite 302
Arlington, VA 22201
703-524-7600
800-950-6264
www.nami.org

Federation of Families for Children's Mental Health
703-684-7710
www.ffcmh.org.

National Institute Of Mental Health (NIMH)
Public Information Branch
5600 Fishers Lane
Rockville, MD 20857
301-443-4515
800-421-4211

American Psychiatric Association
1400 K Street, NW
Washington, DC 20005
202-682-6000

Depression and Related Affective Disorders Association (DRADA)
Johns Hopkins Hospital
Meyer 3-181, 600 North Wolfe Street
Baltimore, MD 21287-7381
410-955-4647

Center for Mental Health Services
5600 Fishers Lane
Rockville, MD 20857
301-443-0001
Fax: 301-443-2792

MENTAL HEALTH PROFESSIONS*

Here are some common mental health professions, with a brief sketch of the education and experience required for each license. Sketches also include general information about reimbursement and restrictions on practice. Note that most professionals have general licenses that allow them to work with any client. Ask the individual about his or her training and experience with "serious mental disorders," because many focus their work on counseling people with "problems of living." Many good psychotherapists

* The information in the following section is quoted from Ruth Czirr's article, "Sorting Out the Mental Health Professions," published by Professional Counseling Associates in February 1994.

are naïve about brain-based disorders,and many physicians prescribe medications without offering rehabilitative services. It's important to look at individual expertise in addition to the person's degree and license.

Psychologists have a doctoral degree. This is often a PhD ("doctor of philosophy," which includes a research program) but includes others such as a PsyD ("doctor of psychology," which has less emphasis on research) or an EdD ("doctor of education"). To be licensed for clinical practice, psychologists must have completed all degree requirements and an internship of one year of intensively supervised practice. Psychologists can practice independently and can be reimbursed by most third-party payers. (Four years college, four to six years graduate school including master's work, dissertation or equivalent, one year internship, possibly one to two years "postdoc" or postdoctoral work.)

Many states also license people who have master's degrees in psychology, using titles such as *Psychological Examiner* or *Psychological Associate*. They must have enough coursework and practicum hours in specific areas to satisfy the breadth requirements and clinical requirements of the law—not all master's programs qualify. They can provide some services independently and others under the supervision of a licensed psychologist. They tend to have difficulty getting reimbursed by third party payers unless they practice as part of a treatment team. (Four years college, two years graduate school, six months internship.)

Psychiatrists are physicians (MDs) who specialize in mental disorders. This is the only profession in most states licensed to prescribe medications and physical treatments. All medical students receive a little training in psychiatry. Legally, any physician can practice psychiatry. However, most physicians who practice psychiatry have completed a three-year residency in psychiatry after medical school. (Compared to the other professions, they have thousands of hours of study in medicine and relatively brief training in other types of assessment and in psychotherapy.) Some go on to become board-certified psychiatrists, which means they have completed a psychiatric residency, practiced for at least two years, and passed an extensive examination.

Psychiatrists (and physicians in general) are the most likely to be reimbursed of all professions, and have the fewest legal restrictions on the scope of their practice. (Four years college, three years medical school, three years residency, possibly one to two years postdoc.)

Social Workers usually have master's degrees in social work and have completed field placements during training. They may specialize in areas such as psychotherapy, medical disorders, community organization, or administration. Most states recognize two levels of graduate licensure in social work. An LMSW (Licensed Master Social Worker) has a master's degree and has passed an examination. An LCSW (Licensed Certified Social Worker) has practiced for two years under supervision as an LMSW and has passed an additional examination.

In some states, a person with a bachelor's degree in social work can be licensed as a BSW or an LSW (Licensed Social Worker). Many LSWs do casework in agencies such as welfare offices or child abuse offices. Doctoral degrees in social work are also offered by some schools. These usually lead to careers in research or college teaching, although some doctoral social workers administer programs and/or have clinical licenses.

LCSWs can be reimbursed by CHAMPUS (the military health insurance program) and Medicare, but many insurance programs still resist paying them except as part of a treatment team. Less highly certified social workers have fewer options for reimbursement. (Four years college for LSW, additional two years graduate school and field placements for LMSW, additional two years supervised experience for LCSW.)

Most states license other counselors with a master's degree, EdS (Educational Specialist), or a doctoral degree in counseling. They have titles such as "Licensed Professional Counselor," or "Marriage, Family, and Child Counselor." They can practice in the specific areas in which they are trained. Some can be reimbursed by CHAMPUS or other payers. For their first few years after graduation, they may have a different title (such as "Licensed Associate Counselors" or LACs) and must practice under supervision. There is a lot of variation from state to state, and you may need to ask for more information. (Education and specialization vary widely; minimum of four years college, two years graduate school, appropriate field placements, two years supervised experience at LAC level before applying for LPC.)

Psychiatric Nurses are usually Registered Nurses with some psychiatric training. Some have a master's degree in psychiatric nursing. They can be reimbursed as part of a treatment team and often work with severely mentally ill people. Because of the shortage of psychiatric nurses, hospital salaries for nurses usually far exceed what community clinics can pay. (Minimum: Nursing school, RN (Registered Nurse) license; many have a four-year BSN (Bachelor of Science in Nursing); some have an MSN (Master of Science in Nursing) as well. A few states have "expanded practice" laws that allow psychiatric nurse specialists who have considerable additional training and experience to prescribe drugs under the supervision of an MD.)

(There are many categories of medical assistants, licensed practical nurses, and nursing assistants. These usually receive their training in technical colleges or hospital-based programs, and can provide specific services under the supervision of a licensed nurse or physician.)

Certified Paraprofessionals may be called "case managers," "outreach workers," or other titles. "Paraprofessional" used by itself covers many different types of work roles and is not a regulated term. They help severely mentally ill adults or children manage their daily lives and obtain the services they need from other agencies. For most of these people, good case management is critical to keeping them well enough to function in the community and stay out of the hospital. These people work under professional supervision as part of a treatment team in a mental health agency; they are sometimes reimbursed by Medicaid and other sources. (Training varies, from high school to four years college, plus a short training course and/or an examination.)

Within the school system, many professionals work as "school counselors" and "school psychology specialists." These are job titles rather than licenses. Typically, these groups receive certification through the State Department of Education. School psychology work includes psychoeducational evaluation, behavioral consultation, and related services done in a school setting. Some school psychology specialists also have a license from the Psychology board.

Students in most professional programs must do clinical work under supervision as part of their training. Students may have titles such as "intern," "practicum student," or "resident." Students are allowed to perform clinical functions appropriate to their level of expertise, supervised according to licensure requirements and good professional practice. (Some of these students already have one of the licenses listed above and are working on a more advanced degree. Others may qualify for certification as a Paraprofessional.)

OTHER TITLES AND CERTIFICATIONS

Unregulated titles. You may encounter other titles that are not legally regulated by the state, including "counselor," "Christian counselor," "pastoral counselor," "hypnotist," "hypnotherapist," "sex therapist," "therapist," "psychotherapist," "psychoanalyst," or even highly individual titles such as "cosmic consciousness counselor."

In most states any person can use titles such as these, no matter what training or lack of training they have. (People who are trained and licensed in one of the professions already described might use some terms like these *in addition to their licensed title* to describe what they do more specifically.) People who have no license but use these titles alone are almost never reimbursed by third-party payers. However, sometimes they are paid by clients directly, or they may work on the staff of a church, hospital, or agency. (Such people usually would not be eligible to work in a community mental health center, because they are not qualified mental health professionals as defined by Medicaid regulations in most states.)

Unregulated practice is possible as long as the person does not misrepresent his or her title or deliver a service that is reserved to a licensed group (such as prescribing medication or giving psychological tests). However, people practicing in such legal gaps are still open to malpractice and negligence suits, and can be in serious trouble if their assessment or intervention leads to a bad outcome.

There are a number of national groups that offer registration or certification for titles such as those just described. Some of these are loosely-organized interest groups that will issue a certificate to any applicant as soon as a fee is paid. Others have a very rigorous credentialing process with stringent requirements for experience and qualifications.

The letters "PA" or "PC" after a professional's name do not denote a degree or a license (or even political correctness). They simply mean that for legal or tax purposes the person's practice or business is organized as a "professional association" or "professional corporation."

GLOSSARY

When I first learned about Kristy's bipolar disorder, I was not familiar with all of the medical terms. The following glossary is a list of words and definitions that may help you better understand your doctor or your loved one's doctor when s/he is explaining the illness to you. Cross-references to other words are *italicized*.

acetylcholine: A type of *neurotransmitter* released by all *neurons* that controls the activity of the skeletal muscles, heartbeat, some glandular functions, mood, sleep, and memory. It is essential to the transmission of brain/spinal cord messages. See *cholinergic*.

acting out: Expressing feelings in actions rather than words, usually without the person being aware of why he or she is doing it. (E.g., the passive-aggressive person "acts out" by dawdling rather than directly saying, "I don't want to do that.")

acute disorder: A disorder that is a change from the person's "normal self." Can usually be helped by counseling, psychotherapy, and/or medical treatment.

adherence: The degree to which the client follows the prescribed course of medication administration. It is used as an alternative term to "compliance," which has overtones of client passivity and obedience, and "noncompliance," which has overtones of deviancy.

affect: Behavior that expresses a subjectively experienced feeling state (emotion); "affect" is responsive to changing emotional states, whereas "mood" refers to a pervasive sustained emotion. Common affects are euphoria, anger, and sadness. "Affective" is the adjective form.

affective disorders: A broad group of disorders whose hallmark is disturbed mood, including severe *depressions*, schizoaffective disorder, *bipolar* disorders, and less severe *chronic* depressions.

agitation: "Revved up" behavior such as pacing, fidgeting, an inability to sit still, handwringing, very rapid talking, or an inability to stop talking. (*Anxiety* is an internal feeling; agitation is a visible behavior.)

agoraphobia: An anxiety disorder in which people are afraid of the world outside a personal "safety zone" such as their neighborhood, house, or even bedroom, or are afraid of being in public places or crowds.

agranulocytosis: A dramatic decrease in the number of infection-fighting white blood cells. Agranulocytosis is a very rare side effect of *antipsychotic drugs*, most notably of *Clozapine*. Even in the case of *Clozapine*, it is said to afflict only one to two percent of users, and the ill effects of this disease can be reversed if it is identified early and use of the drugs discontinued.

akathisia: Complaints of restlessness accompanied by movements such as fidgeting the legs, rocking from foot to foot, pacing, or an inability to sit or stand. Symptoms develop within a few weeks of starting or raising the dose of a *neuroleptic* medication or of reducing the dose of medication used to treat *extrapyramidal symptoms*.

akinesia: A state of motor inhibition; reduced voluntary movement.

alexithymia: Literally, "no words for feelings." Person talks entirely in terms of thoughts and actions, seems blank or puzzled if you push for information about emotions.

alogia: Literally, "speechlessness." Most commonly used to refer to the lack of spontaneity in speech and diminished flow of conversation that occur as negative *symptoms* in schizophrenia.

amygdala: In the structure of the brain, part of the *basal ganglia*. As an important component of the *limbic system*, it is most consistently linked with emotional reactivity, basic learning, and memory processes.

anhedonia: An inability to experience pleasure or any positive feelings; no pleasurable reaction to good events. An overpowering loss of interest in what used to be pleasant.

anorexia: Loss of appetite; a common symptom of *depression*, bereavement, and other conditions.

anorexia nervosa: A psychiatric disorder with a key *symptom* of refusal to eat.

anti-anxiety drug: Drugs such as Valium and Xanax which dull *anxiety* and reduce its physical manifestations such as body tension. Most create a temporary pleasant feeling in normal people, and there is some danger that they may be abused or that some people may become dependent on them. Also called "minor tranquilizers."

anticholinergic: Side effects or adverse effects that result from the suppressive action of certain *antipsychotic* and *antidepressant* medications on the action of *acetylcholine* in the brain and peripheral nervous system. The actual side effects include dry mouth, blurred vision, constipation, and urinary hesitancy.

antidepressant drug: Several types of drugs which normalize brain chemistry to counteract depressive *symptoms*. Also help some *anxiety* disorders and eating disorders. Not a stimulant that makes one "happy." If a non-depressed person takes it, it may have no effect or only side effects such as drowsiness.

antipsychotic drug: Any drug which normalizes brain chemistry to control psychotic symptoms. If non-psychotic people take it, it has only side effects such as intense drowsiness. Also called "major tranquilizers" or "*neuroleptics*." Also prescribed for a few other medical and psychiatric disorders.

anxiety: Apprehension, tension, or uneasiness.

anxiolytics: Drugs that have an anti-anxiety effect and are used widely to relieve emotional tension. The most commonly used anti-anxiety drugs are the *benzodiazepines*.

autonomic nervous system: Regulates the involuntary process of the internal organs and blood vessels. Many of the functions controlled by the autonomic nervous system are self-regulating or "autonomous." It is comprised of two primary sub-systems: the *sympathetic* and parasympathetic systems, which sometimes work in cooperation but other times are antagonistic in their contrasting roles of "arousal" and "rest." Operates outside of consciousness but can be dramatically affected by emotions, stress, or psychiatric disorders (e.g., producing heart palpitations, shortness of breath, or diarrhea when anxious).

axon: A nerve-fiber projection from the *neuron* that serves to transmit to adjacent neurons. *Neurotransmitter* substances are contained within an axon. The axon terminal (or end) is also the site of the neurotransmitter release.

basal ganglia: Structures located on both sides of the *limbic system*, involved in the regulation of movement and in a variety of neuropsychiatric symptoms including *dementia*, major *depression*, and *psychosis*. Contains the caudale nucleus, the key area of the brain involved in learning and breaking habits.

behavioral therapy, behavior therapy: A type of psychotherapy that essentially concentrates on a person's actions, using techniques such as relaxation training, observing and counting behaviors, and deliberately learning new behavior. The techniques and treatment plan can be quite sophisticated, and this general type of therapy is particularly effective with problems including *anxiety* disorders, behavioral *symptoms* in mentally retarded people, and many problems of childhood.

benzodiazepines: The generic name for a group of drugs that have potent hypnotic, sedative, and anxiolytic action. They are also called *anxiolytics* or *anti-anxiety drugs*.

beta blockers: Refers to a class of drugs that reduces *anxiety* by blocking the beta receptors in the *autonomic nervous system*. They block those receptors that stimulate heartbeat and those that dilate blood vessels and air channels in the lungs. They are as strong as *benzodiazepines*, despite the greater dosages needed, and they are not addictive. They are, however, short-acting and do not remain long in the system. They are most effective for specific situations of unmanageable *anxiety*.

biological psychiatry: A school of psychiatric thought that emphasizes physical, chemical, and neurological causes of psychiatric illnesses and treatment approaches.

bipolar disorder: A disorder with episodes of *mania* and usually also of *depression*.

bizarre: Very seriously *irrational*; you couldn't show this in a movie without using special effects. (E.g., "My nerves are rotting inside my muscles and the worms are eating them.")

boundary: The sense of personal integrity and separateness between two or more people. In everyday life we set boundaries by actions such as keeping information private, closing the bathroom door, or recognizing that friends can disagree. Children gradually learn that each person is a separate being, that everybody doesn't experience the same thing at the same time, and that people do not have a right to invade others' bodies or minds without consent. Healthy adults are able to set different boundaries in different relationships (e.g., having sex with your spouse but not with friends or children; being frank with a friend but cautious with a reporter).

boundaries, disturbed: People with emotional disorders or immature characters often have personal or family *boundaries* that are too rigid (letting no one in), too loose (letting anyone in), or too variable (feeling out of control and jumping from one extreme to the other) and may be confused about whom a feeling or thought belongs to (e.g., "I'm cold. Put on your sweater;" or a client who feels sexually aroused or angry but denies those feelings and accuses the therapist of having them). Psychotherapy often works to make a person's (or an entire family's) boundaries more comfortable and *functional*.

catatonic behavior: Marked motor abnormalities, generally limited to those occurring as part of a psychotic disorder. This term includes catatonic excitement (apparently purposeless agitation not influenced by external stimuli), stupor (decreased reactivity and fewer spontaneous movements, often with apparent unawareness of surroundings), negativism (apparent motiveless resistance to instructions or attempts to be moved), posturing (assuming and maintaining an inappropriate or bizarre stance), rigidity (maintaining a stance of posture against all efforts to be moved), and waxy flexibility (the person's limbs can be put into positions that are maintained).

central nervous system (CNS): The brain and the spinal cord.

cerebral cortex: The upper portion of the brain consisting of layers of *neurons* and pathways connecting them. The cerebral cortex is divided into four lobes on each side and is the part of the brain responsible for higher-order thinking and decision making.

cerebrospinal fluid (CSF): Fluid manufactured in the brain and contained within the brain and spinal cord; it circulates in the *central nervous system*.

character disorder: A disorder which has been present for the person's entire adult life and which represents a basic stunting or failure in the development of mature traits and capabilities such as responsibility, flexibility, or empathy. The person has *chronic*, habitual, maladaptive *defenses* that are not flexible, limit the person's potential, and cause problems for other people. The person is usually self-satisfied and feels little need for change.

cholinergic: Activated by acetylcholine, this is the part of the *autonomic nervous system* that controls the life-sustaining organs of the body.

chronic: Any condition or disorder that continues over a long period of time, especially if it continues despite treatment. Chronic conditions often begin inconspicuously, and *symptoms* may be less pronounced than in acute conditions.

chronically mentally ill: See *Serious Mental Illness*.

Clozapine (Clozaril): An antipsychotic drug found effective in severe and persistent schizophrenia. It is not used as a first-line antipsychotic because it produces a small risk of *agranulocytosis*, a depletion of white blood cells that can be fatal if not monitored. Clozapine has demonstrated effectiveness in treating the positive and negative *symptoms* of schizophrenia.

co-dependent: A person who is in an intimate relationship with a substance abuser and is emotionally caught up in the abuser's problems and whose behavior unknowingly helps the abuser continue.

cognition: Thought, reasoning, logical sequences. "Cognitive" is the adjective form.

cognitive therapy: A broad type of psychotherapy that concentrates on the relationship between people's thoughts, emotions, and perceptions, using techniques such as making written records of thoughts, tracing *dysfunctional* thought patterns, and testing beliefs about other people. In its simplest form it may be thought of as applying *behavioral therapy* to actions that occur inside the brain; in its most complex form it verges on *psychodynamic psychotherapy*, tracing the development of distorted thought patterns to the experiences earlier in life which formed them.

comorbidity: The occurrence of two or more disorders at the same time. The disorders may occur independently of each other, or one may occur as a consequence of the other. See *dual diagnosis*.

compulsion: Insistent, repetitive, *intrusive*, and unwanted urge to do some action; acting on an *obsession*. (E.g., because of obsessive worry about her children's safety, a mother is compelled to call her babysitter twice every hour.)

confidentiality: The ethical principle that a physician may not reveal any information disclosed in the course of medical attendance.

congenital: Present at birth, perhaps due to genetics, to prenatal injury, or to birth injury.

countertransference: The reactions of a counselor toward a particular client triggered by something about the client but growing out of the counselor's personal history. (E.g., a counselor whose mother was very depressed may feel helpless and fearful around depressed clients.) Can interfere with good counseling if not recognized; if noticed and explored, it can provide valuable clues to the client's problems. (See also *transference*.)

decompensation, decompensate: The crumbling of usual *defenses* in a person who is moving toward a *psychotic break*. This word is sometimes incorrectly used to describe a person who is temporarily overcome by emotion, especially if the therapist is nervous around strong emotions.

defense: Technique a person uses to control uncomfortable feelings or avoid a painful or frightening truth; this process is outside of the person's awareness. *Magical thinking, denial, dissociation*, and *repression* are a few examples. All humans use defenses to some degree; the more rigid, inappropriate, unrealistic, and *dysfunctional* they are, the more likely the person has some *character disorder*.

deinstitutionalization: Change in locus of mental health care from traditional, institutional settings to community-based services. Sometimes called trans-institutionalization because it often merely shifts the patients from one institution (the hospital) to another (such as a prison).

delirium: *Organic* brain syndrome such as *paranoia* or memory loss that is the direct result of a medical illness, injury, poisoning, etc., and that would go away if the medical cause were found and corrected before permanent damage occurs. On casual observation, can easily be confused with *dementia*, leading to failure to treat.

delusion: A false belief that the person firmly holds despite obvious proof and unarguable evidence against it. This false belief is not held in common by the rest of the person's cultural group. (E.g., delusion of being controlled by some outside force; delusions of grandeur [godlike powers or importance]; delusional persecution [being singled out for pursuit or harm]; *somatic* delusions [strange things happening in body, severe distortion in body image].)

dementia: Any serious, permanent, *progressive, organic* brain syndrome, with memory loss as a key symptom. "Demented" is the adjective form.

dendrite: The short extension of the *neuron* that is the neuron's "receiving end" for signals sent from other cells; it is located close to the *axons* of other cells separated by a short distance from the synaptic cleft.

denial: A primitive *defense*. "I didn't do that," or "It never happened," when, in fact,the person did do it or the thing did happen.

depersonalization: Feelings of unreality or strangeness concerning either the environment, the self, or both. This is characteristic of depersonalization disorder and may also occur in schizotypal personality disorder, schizophrenia, and in those persons experiencing overwhelming *anxiety*, stress, or fatigue. (See also *Derealization*.)

depression: May refer to a sad, despairing, or discouraged mood (often a normal feeling state). Depressive disorders are a combination of *cognitive*, *somatic*, and *affective symptoms* with a *dysphoric* mood that is usually, but not always, depressed.

derealization: A feeling of estrangement from one's environment; "It was like watching a movie," "It was like walking through a dream." Like *depersonalization*, this can be experienced by anyone during a traumatic event (e.g., accident), or can be a *symptom* of various disorders.

dexamethasone-suppression test (DST): A test of hormone function sometimes used as a diagnostic tool in *depression*. In healthy individuals, the administration of dexamethasone suppresses the concentration of cortisol in the blood. Approximately forty to fifty percent of persons diagnosed with major depression have an abnormal DST in that they do not suppress cortisol in response to dexamethasone.

diagnosis: Systematic process of "ruling out" a series of possible mental disorders until the disorder that best explains the *symptoms* is found. The legal implication of stating a diagnosis is that the professional has eliminated the possibility of all disorders more serious than the one named, including *organic* causes. Diagnosis often includes more than one disorder, often an *acute disorder* overlaid on a *character disorder* or in combination with medical conditions.

differential diagnosis: The consideration of which of two or more diseases with similar symptoms the patient suffers from. (E.g., if the person's most prominent symptom is confused thinking, the differential diagnosis might be between drug intoxication, *dementia*, *delirium*, *psychosis*, and very severe *depression*.) Failure to consider the differential diagnoses can lead to severe errors in choice of treatment.

disorientation: Person is confused about his or her own physical location, location in time, or who is present. A serious symptom, often of *psychosis* or *organic* brain disorders.

dissociation: A *defense* in which emotions are separated and detached from an idea or situation.

dopamine: A *neurotransmitter* which regulates movement, mood, and motivation. There are three major pathways in the brain's dopamine system: 1) mesocortical: emotion, motivation, cognition; 2) mesolimbic: feelings, emotions, *psychosis*; 3) nigostriatal: planned and voluntary coordination of movement.

dopamine hypothesis: A theory that attempts to explain the pathogenesis of schizophrenia and other psychotic states due to excesses in *dopamine* activity in various areas of the brain. The theory is, in part, based on biological observations that the *antipsychotic* properties of specific drugs may be related to their ability to block the action of dopamine, and the opposite effects of stimulants that increase the action of dopamine.

DSM-IV: Diagnostic and Statistical Manual of Mental Disorders, 4th Edition, 1994. The American Psychiatric Association's official classification of mental disorders.

dual diagnosis: The co-occurrence within one's lifetime of a psychiatric disorder and a substance use disorder. *Comorbidity* is the preferred term.

dynamic therapy: Usually used to mean *insight-oriented psychotherapy*; sometimes means *psychodynamic psychotherapy*.

dysfunctional, dysfunction: Not functional, not working well or correctly; process or symptom that causes problems for a person in relationships, at work, or with the ability to cope with everyday life. (E.g., impotence is a sexual dysfunction; people with *character disorders* have dysfunctional behavior, although they may feel no subjective distress; an adolescent may find that her high intelligence is socially dysfunctional among her less intelligent classmates.)

dyskinesia: Any disturbance of movement. It may also be induced by medication.

dysphoria: Unpleasant mood; usually a sad mood but also irritability, *anhedonia*, etc. "Dysphoric" is adjective form.

dystonia: Abnormal positioning or spasm of the muscles of the head, neck, or limbs; the dystonia develops within a few days of starting or raising the doseage of a *neuroleptic* medication, because of dysfunction of the *extrapyramidal system.*

efficacy: Effectiveness of a drug as a therapeutic agent, particularly over long-term use.

ego: In modern psychology, the set of abilities a child gradually acquires to cope with the world. Includes a sense of identity and self, *reality-testing,* perceptual and logical skills; the ability to manage emotions and delay gratification; the ability to understand others and take responsibility for self. A person with "good ego strength" can use all these functions naturally and flexibly, even under stress. A person with "poor ego strength" may have only limited use of these functions, use what they have rigidly or inappropriately, and *decompensate* under stress. (Should not be confused with the popular use of "ego," which connotes selfishness or maladaptive focus on the self; professionals use "*narcissistic*" that for concept.)

ego-dystonic: Action, thought, or feeling which is at odds with the person's own self-image and conscious intentions. (E.g., "That just wasn't like me;" in a person with a mature character, casual shoplifting would be very ego-dystonic.)

ego-syntonic: The opposite of *ego-dystonic.* Action, thought, or feeling that is congruent with the person's own self-image and conscious intentions. (E.g., in a person with an antisocial personality disorder, stealing from family members can be completely ego-syntonic, despite the fact that it harms them.)

electroconvulsive therapy (ECT): The use of electric currents, with anesthetics and muscle relaxants, applied briefly to one or both sides of the brain. Most effective in severe *depression.*

electroencephalograph: An instrument for measuring electrical waves generated by *neurons* in the brain.

empathy: Degree to which a person can understand others' dilemmas and points of view and "feel with" their emotional condition. Empathy is one component of successful intervention, but additional skills are usually needed to effect change in people with problems or disorders.

episode: A period of psychiatric disorder. (E.g., a person may be mildly depressed throughout adult life, but have several episodes of major depressive disorder that require hospitalization.) Serious disorders may leave *residual* symptoms between episodes.

euphoria: An exaggerated feeling of physical and emotional well-being; extremely happy mood; when a person is so happy or giddy as to seem intoxicated. "Euphoric" is adjective form.

euthymic mood state: A generally positive mood state, or emotional wellness, marked by the absence of *chronic* or serious mood disorders, which might affect social functioning negatively.

exacerbation: Worsening of symptom or disorder. (E.g., scolding people and telling them to "shape up" can exacerbate *depression*; treatment with intensive *psychodynamic psychotherapy* can exacerbate *psychotic* disorders.)

extrapyramidal symptoms (EPS): A variety of *sign* symptoms, including muscular rigidity, tremors, drooling, shuffling *gait*, restlessness (*akathisia*), peculiar involuntary postures (*dystonia*), motor inertia (*akinesia*), and many other neurological disturbances. Results from *dysfunction* of the extrapyramidal system. May occur as a side effect of certain *psychotropic* drugs, particularly *neuroleptics*.

flight of ideas: *Psychotic* symptoms in which person rapidly skips from one idea to another based on unusual associations such as puns or highly personalized links. Often seen in *manic episodes*.

formulary: A list of specific drugs approved by an insurer, sometimes including the specific illnesses the drug may be used to treat. Drugs that are not on the formulary may not be paid for at all, or may require some sort of prior authorization or other special procedure before they will be covered.

fugue, fugue state: A traumatic stress reaction in which the person loses all memory of stressful events and travels away from home while suffering this amnesia.

functional: 1. Well-suited to the person's environment; behavior that helps relieve a problem or helps a person fit in.

(E.g., "His phobias upset him, but they are also functional because his wife is more affectionate when he's frightened;" "Her single-mindedness and indifference to social contact are really pretty functional in her job writing computer programs.") 2. In technical writing, may be used to mean "not *organic*." (E.g., "Since tests have eliminated all possible physical causes, I think his pain must be functional.")

GABA **(gama aminobutyric acid)**: An amino acid and *neurotransmitter* throughout the *central nervous system* that has a vital dampening effect on the excitability of nerve cells.

gait: Way of walking. (E.g., a depressed person may have a shuffling, dragging gait; a *manic* person may have a prancing, rapid gait; a stroke patient may have an unbalanced, cautious gait with one side dragging after the other.)

gender identity: The inner, *cognitive* sense of one's maleness or femaleness which is part of the person's "self;" this is a more fundamental process than the development of sexual attraction to males or females. While anatomical sex is obvious at birth unless the person has an unusual *congenital* defect, gender identity develops slowly over the early years of childhood. It may develop inconsistently due to very disturbed parenting or may become disturbed during adult life in severe *psychotic* disorders (e.g., a psychotic woman may believe that she has grown a penis).

genes: Located at various points along the chromosomes, genes are bits of deoxyribonucleic acid (DNA) that carry the hereditary code. It is estimated that a human has approximately a hundred thousand genes, known collectively as the genome.

glial cells: "Glue cells." Glial cells are small *neurons* that are specialized to provide nourishment and support for the command neurons located in gray matter regions such as the cortex or the *basal ganglia*.

glutamate: A *neurotransmitter*; an amino acid governing much of human thought and emotion, regulating systems involved in cognitive and higher mental functions (memory, learning, sensory reception, information processing). Glutamate serves as the brain's major excitatory neurotransmitter, causing *neurons* to "fire" rather than cease firing. Glutamate is also the sole source of *GABA*, the predominant inhibitor in the *CNS*.

grandiosity: Exaggerated belief or claims of one's importance of identity, often manifested by delusions of great wealth, power, or fame.

hallucination: Sensory experience not based on reality. Hearing, seeing, tasting, smelling, or feeling something that isn't there. Most commonly involves hearing, which is experienced as noises OUTSIDE head, coming through ears. (See also *pseudohallucinations*.)

hippocampus: A *nucleus* in the brain crucial to learning and term memory; part of the *limbic system*.

hyper-: Prefix showing extreme or exaggerated amount. (E.g., hypervigilance is constant scanning and exaggerated attention to the environment.)

hypersomnia: Sleeping more than is normal for the person; opposite of *insomnia*.

hypertensive crisis: Sudden and sometimes fatal rise in blood pressure; it may occur as a result of combining monoamine oxidase inhibitors and tyramine in food or over-the-counter medications (e.g., cough remedies and nose drops).

hypo-: Prefix showing inadequate amount or small amount. (E.g., hypomanic episodes are similar to *manic* episodes but much less severe.)

hypothalamus: The complex brain structure composed of many nuclei with various functions. It is the head ganglion of the *autonomic nervous system* and is involved in the control of heat regulation, heart rate, blood pressure, respiration, sexual activity, digestion, appetite, body weight, wakefulness, fight or flight response, rage and water, fat, and carbohydrate metabolism.

iatrogenic: Harmful effects presumed to be caused (inadvertently) by the treatment itself.

illusion: A misperception of a real external stimulus.

insight: Degree to which individuals can accurately describe themselves, their emotional processes, their problems, their strengths, and their weaknesses. The ability to perceive and face truths about oneself; a person with mature *defenses* has good insight.

insight-oriented psychotherapy: Broad term for many different types of therapy which aim to increase individuals' conscious awareness and understanding of their behavior and emotions, in part by systematically exposing and breaking down their *defenses*, in part by recalling significant events and influences in their childhood. Helpful for some mental disorders and for many people's problems in living; seldom helpful for *character disorders*; may *exacerbate* psychotic disorders by triggering *decompensation*. (Sometimes loosely referred to as *dynamic* or *psychodynamic psychotherapy*, often by practitioners with very little training in psychodynamic theory and practice.)

insomnia: The inability to fall asleep (also called initial insomnia), or stay asleep (also called middle insomnia), or waking up too early (also called terminal insomnia or early morning wakening).

intrusive thoughts: Unwelcome thoughts that interrupt normal thought processes and cannot be driven out.

irrational: Not logical, not supported by reality.

kindling: The creation of seizures in an area of the brain by subjecting repeated, low-level electrical stimulation; eventually the area becomes so sensitive that seizures will occur spontaneously, with no electrical stimulus.

lability: Rapid shifts in emotions; very unstable emotions. "Labile" is adjective form.

limbic system: A network of structures in the forebrain (including the *hippocampus*, *amygdala*, thalamus, and *hypothalamus*) that work to regulate human emotions such as fear, anger, *depression*, excitement, and certain aspects of movement; regulates emotion, memory, arousal, cognition.

lithium: Used in the treatment of acute mania and as a maintenance medication to help reduce the duration, intensity, and frequency of *bipolar disorder*. There is a narrow band of effective dosage above which toxicity occurs and below which there is no effect; can also cause fetal damage.

loose associations: *Psychotic* symptom in which ideas shift from one subject to another in a random or unrelated manner. The speaker is unaware of the looseness; if severe, speech becomes incoherent.

magical thinking: A childlike *defense*; conviction that thought alone causes an event. Normal in young children; it can occur in adults under severe stress or in those with mental disorders. (E.g., "My father had a heart attack because I was mad at him and wished he was dead.")

maintenance drug therapy: Continuing a therapeutic drug after it has reached its maximum *efficacy*, and at a minimum effective level to prevent a relapse of the illness.

mania, manic symptoms, manic episode: The "high" portion of a *bipolar disorder*.

"maniac": Non-professional, vague, sensational word for an emotionally disturbed person. Implies violence. Sometimes confused with "*manic*" by the public.

manic-depressive: An older term roughly equivalent to what is called *bipolar disorder* today.

mental retardation: Deficiencies in intellectual and *cognitive* functioning, usually with an *organic* cause, often present at birth. When used as a diagnosis, this broad category has very different implications depending on the severity of the deficiencies (e.g., persons with mild mental retardation may be able to live independently and be self-supporting; at the opposite extreme, persons with severe and profound mental retardation may be incontinent, incapable of understanding speech, or unable to sit up without assistance). This is different from *motor retardation*, which is a *symptom* of *depression* and other emotional disorders.

metabolite: A compound that results from the chemical breakdown of a *neurotransmitter* in the space between nerve cells (*synapse*).

narcissistic: *Character disorder* or trait which includes feeling grandiosely self-important, demanding attention and admiration, wanting to seem godlike, or becoming enraged if doubted or criticized.

"nerves": Non-professional, vague word often used to describe *anxiety*, but people may use it to describe almost any *symptom*. Always ask for details!

"nervous breakdown": Non-professional word for any emotional problem severe enough to keep the person from functioning adequately; might be used to describe a *psychotic break* or perhaps severe *depression*; sometimes just a temper outburst or a protracted pout. Always ask for details!

neuroleptic: Referring to a specific effect of a pharmacologic age the nervous system; specifically a drug whose principal effect is on psychomotor activity.

neurons: Nerve cells which carry information processing in the brain.

neuroscience: The study of brain function, the neural substrates of behavior and how the nervous system is affected by disease.

neurosis, neurotic: Popular word, not a *diagnosis* but referring to a disorder which distresses the person but is not severe enough to be psychotic (that is, does not severely disturb the person's *reality-testing* and other usual *ego* functions). Also used to differentiate from *character disorders*, in which the disorder is the person's "normal self" and the person feels little or no distress.

neurotransmitters: Chemicals normally found in the brain that form the physical basis for processes of memory, *affect*, and *cognition*. Disturbances and imbalances in neurotransmitter functioning have been found in several severe psychiatric disorders and *organic* syndromes.

norepinephrine: A type of *neurotransmitter* secreted by the adrenal glands in response to arousal-provoking events such as stress. It influences emotional behavior, alertness, *anxiety* and tension.

nucleus: In the minute structure of a typical cell, the nucleus is a denser body in its midst. It represents the directive center of most cellular activities, governing the process of cell division and hereditary transmission.

obsession: Persistent, *intrusive* thought or impulse that cannot be eliminated by logic or pushed out of awareness by an act of will. May have content, such as "My baby is in danger," or may seem meaningless, such as silently saying the alphabet over and over. If acted upon, they become *compulsions*.

organic: Very broad term for any disorder that is caused directly by a physical injury, birth defect, or disease that damages the brain. Depending on the disorder and its location in the brain, damage may be mild or severe; its effects may be permanent or, with rehabilitation, the brain may be able to recover or replace some of its lost functions.

paranoia: A severe, unrealistic, often psychotic form of suspiciousness; disorder or *symptom* involving *delusions* that the person is harassed, pursued, harmed, or sexually betrayed. Often the person misinterprets insignificant actual events to fit a complex and elaborate delusional system (e.g., when in reality he has dialed a wrong number, a paranoid person thinks that the FBI and French security forces are intercepting his phone calls, which also explains the poor reception he has been getting on his TV). Paranoid people usually also believe they are endowed with unique and superior abilities or importance.

parietal lobe: A physically distinct area of the *cerebral cortex* responsible for the intellectual processing of sensory information (visual, tactile, auditory) and also responsible for verbal and visual-spatial processing.

peptides, neuropeptides: Chemicals, including some hormones, that act as messengers in the brain and modulate the activity of many other *neurotransmitters*.

perceptual: *Sensory* and *cognitive* skills involved in noticing, paying attention to, choosing from, and interpreting events and messages. (E.g., a husband's description of his wife tells you his perceptions of her and may or may not be an accurate description of how she feels or behaves.) See *hallucinations* and *pseudo-hallucinations*, which are both perceptions that do not match outside stimuli.

personality disorder: See *character disorder*.

prodromal phase: The phase during which a deteriorating state of health that later culminates in full-blown illness is recognized. During the deterioration phase, there are subtle warning signs of the impending illness, such as withdrawal, bizarre thoughts, or other behaviors recognized as precursors of a *psychotic episode.*

prognosis: An individual's prospect for recovery, based on knowledge of the usual course of the disorder and the circumstances of a particular case.

progressive: Any disorder which will continue to worsen over time. (E.g., the loss of brain function in Alzheimer's disease may happen slowly or rapidly, but it will inevitably get worse.)

prophylactic: A treatment or medication used to protect against the onset or recurrence of a disease or disorder.

pseudohallucinations: Perceptions (usually sounds or visions) that superficially resemble *hallucinations* but are caused by more normal processes. They may be *perceptual* distortions of a real stimulus, such as seeing the shadow of a limb and thinking it is an animal. Any person may experience pseudohallucinations while falling asleep or while awakening, and brief pseudohallucinations of seeing or hearing a dead person are common during the first year of normal grief reactions.

psychodynamic psychotherapy: School of therapy based on the theories of Freud and his disciples in which the therapist slowly penetrates the patient's *defenses* to ultimately "work through" unconscious conflicts and reorganize the person's basic character. It relies heavily on *transference* as a way of learning about the patient and of giving the patient new emotional experiences. In psychoanalysis, the most intensive form, therapy occurs several times per week for several years. Few therapists practicing today are trained in this strict method, and many professionals use this term to describe less intensive *insight-oriented psychotherapy.* However, many useful concepts and techniques have been adapted from psychodynamic work and integrated into other types of therapy.

psychomotor agitation: Excessive motor activity, usually nonpurposeful and associated with internal tension. (E.g., the inability to sit still, fidgeting, pacing, wringing of hands, or pulling of clothes.)

psychopharmacology: The study of the action of drugs that affect thinking, emotion, and behavior; the branch of medicine that specializes in medications to treat mental illnesses.

psychosis: A mental state characterized by extreme impairment of the sufferer's perception of reality, including *hallucinations*, *delusions*, incoherence, and *bizarre* behavior, which is so severe that the person cannot meet the ordinary demands of life.

psychotic break, psychotic episode: Period lasting from hours to months during which a person has so many psychotic symptoms that he or she cannot make sense of reality or control thoughts, emotions, and actions. People experiencing a serious break can be unable to care for themselves ("gravely disabled") or may be dangerous to themselves or others.

psychotropic drugs: Drugs that alter psychological functioning and/or mood, thoughts, motor abilities, balance, movement, and coordination.

reality-testing: Clarity of *perceptions*; the ability to evaluate the external world objectively and to tell the difference between external events and personal, internal thoughts and feelings.

receptor/receptor molecule: Protein molecules embedded in the walls of nerve cells that bind *neurotransmitters*. Each receptor binds a specific neurotransmitter, thereby turning particular biochemical or cellular mechanisms on or off. Receptors are generally found in the *dendrite* and cell body of *neurons*.

refractory: Non-response to the known therapeutic effect of a drug or course of drug treatment, or non-response due to increased tolerance to a drug over time. See *treatment resistant*.

rehabilitation: In psychiatry, the methods and techniques used to achieve maximum functioning and optimum adjustment for the patient and to prevent relapses or recurrences of illness; sometimes termed "tertiary prevention."

repression: A *defense* in which something painful is partially or completely "forgotten;" with therapy or other events, the lost memory can be recovered. (E.g., incest survivors repress their conscious ability to recall the attacks they experienced, while continuing to have recurring nightmares about them and to become anxious or fearful in situations related to them.)

residuals, residual phase: A few lingering *symptoms* left over after an *episode* of a disorder ends; changes in personality that linger after major symptoms are controlled. (E.g., schizophrenic people often have residuals such as social anxiety and mild *hallucinations* present even between acute *psychotic episodes*).

retardation, motor retardation: Extremely slowed down behavior such as sitting for minutes without any body motion; very slow speech with long pauses; dragging steps. (Fatigue is an internal feeling; retardation is a visible behavior.) This is a symptom that is not related to the disorders of *mental retardation*.

reuptake: Removal of a *neurotransmitter* from the *synapse* by the *neuron* that released it; reabsorption.

sedation: Giving *antipsychotics* or other drugs to quiet an *agitated* person temporarily.

sensory: Pertaining to input from any of the five senses; the raw material of *perceptions*.

Serious Mental Illness: A legal term for people with serious, disabling, recurrent disorders, such as schizophrenia, who are eligible for special forms of state or federal aid. Usually abbreviated as SMI.

serotonin: A type of *neurotransmitter* that impacts sensory processes, muscular activity, and *cognition*. It is a factor in states of consciousness, basic bodily functions, complex sensory and motor activities, and mood. Serotonin is thought to be implicated in mood disorders, aggression, and schizophrenia. Fluoxetine (Prozac) and *Clozapine (Clozaril)* are thought to be significant effects of the serotonergic systems (those that produce serotonin).

side effect: A drug response that accompanies the principal response for which a medication is taken. Most side effects are undesirable yet cause only minor disturbances; others may cause serious problems.

sign: Objective evidence of disease or disorder. See also *symptom*.

somatic: Pertaining to the physical body. Somatic *symptoms* include sleep and appetite disturbances, fatigue, etc.

somatization: A *defense* in which emotional problems are expressed in physical *symptoms*, often autonomic ones. (E.g., person gets headaches when criticized, develops severe bowel disturbances because of chronic *anxiety*.) People who react with somatization often are unaware of their emotions and strongly focus their attention on the physical symptoms.

splitting: A *defense* usually seen in borderline personality disorder. Rather than struggle to understand and reconcile mixed feelings or complicated information, the person splits others into all-good or all-evil people. (E.g., the only possible reason you might do something that makes me uncomfortable is because you are evil or you hate me.) The person has very little awareness of the see-sawing and may insist that the offender "has always been like this" or "was just fooling me before."

supportive psychotherapy: Roughly, the converse of *insight-oriented therapy*. The counselor provides *empathy* and emotional support, and tries to help people strengthen their accustomed *defenses* to control distress. Helpful in some situations, especially for healthy people coping with a trauma such as bereavement, or people with *Serious Mental Illness* whose symptoms are controlled by medication and who are trying to remain *functional* in daily life to prevent a *psychotic break*. Can sometimes reduce symptoms in some psychiatric disorders, very unlikely to cause improvement in people with *character disorders*.

sympathetic nervous system: The part of the *autonomic nervous system* that responds to dangerous or threatening situations by preparing a person physiologically for "fight or flight."

symptom: A specific manifestation of a patient's condition indicative of an abnormal physical or mental state; a subjective perception of illness.

synapse: The gap between the membrane of one nerve cell and the membrane of another. The synapse is the space through which the nerve impulse is passed chemically or electrically, from one nerve to another.

syndrome: A configuration of symptoms that occur together and constitute a recognizable condition.

systems therapy: Therapy that concentrates on the interactions among a natural group of people, usually a family; there are a number of different schools of thought within this broad group that concentrate on different aspects of family history, roles, or interactions. Usually asks whether psychiatric symptoms in one person are being caused or worsened by dysfunction in the system around them, and treats the group as a working unit. People who identify themselves as systems therapists may work with a small family group, a large group (e.g., several generations in the room at once), or may see a person in individual or couples therapy while "keeping the system in mind."

tachycardia: Unusually rapid heartbeat (greater than one hundred beats per minute) that may result from the side effects of *antidepressants* acting on the *autonomic nervous system*. It is a form of heart arrhythmia.

tactile: Pertaining to the sense of touch (e.g., people in alcoholic withdrawal may have *hallucinations* of bugs crawling on their arms).

tapering: The process of slowly decreasing the dose of medication over several days or weeks until the medication is completely discontinued. This is done to reduce or avoid *withdrawal symptoms*.

tardive dyskinesia: A side effect of traditional antipsychotic drugs. This side effect, which involves abnormal involuntary movements of the face, tongue, mouth, fingers, upper and lower limbs, and occasionally the entire body, usually appears after taking the drug for some time and occurs in at least a mild form in twenty-five to forty percent of patients on antipsychotic agents. Tardive dyskinesia may be severe or irreversible in five to ten percent of cases.

thought disorder: Psychotic disturbance of speech, communication, or the process of thinking.

tolerance: The reduced responsiveness of the body to a drug as a function of reduced sensitivity of the nerve receptors over time.

toxicity: The capacity of a drug to damage body tissue or seriously impair body functions.

tranquilizer: A drug that decreases anxiety and agitation. Preferred terms are *anti-anxiety* and *antipsychotic drugs*.

transference: Reactions of the person toward the counselor, including assumptions about how the counselor thinks and feels about the person. They reflect basic assumptions about the world, learned from the actions of powerful adults in early life. These are highly emotional, seldom conscious, and can be powerful clues to the person's mistaken assumptions and dilemmas in all close relationships. (See also *countertransference*.)

treatment resistant: Lack of response to a specific therapy that would ordinarily be expected to be effective. The patient who does not respond to the usual dosage of a drug but does respond to a higher dosage is often termed a "relative resister." Absolute resistance refers to the patient who fails to respond to any dosage of the drug. See *refractory*.

tremor: A trembling or shaking of the body or any of its parts. It may be induced by medication.

triangulation: A triangle is any relationship among three people (e.g., mother, father, and son; helper, client, and client's husband). In triangulation, two people ally against or shut out the third; or person A uncritically accepts person B's *perceptions* of person C, without getting information directly from person C. A triangulated helper loses objectivity, overlooks important information, and takes sides; he or she will have difficulty causing positive change in the couple, and may only deepen their problems. People with *character disorders* are especially likely to triangulate their helpers, either deliberately or without awareness of what they are doing.

uncovering therapy: See *insight-oriented psychotherapy*.

withdrawal: A pathological retreat from people or the world of reality, often seen in schizophrenia.

withdrawal symptoms: New symptoms that arise because a drug is discontinued. These almost always go away within two weeks of drug discontinuation. *Tapering* a drug rather than abruptly discontinuing it reduces and sometimes even eliminates withdrawal symptoms.

RESOURCES

Beigel, David, Esther Sales, and Richard Schulz. *Family Caregiving in Chronic Illness: Alzheimer's Disease, Cancer, Heart Disease, Mental Illness, Stroke.* Newbury Park, Calif.: Sage, 1991.

Berger, Diane. *We Heard the Angels of Madness: One Family's Struggle with Manic Depression.* N.Y.: William Morrow, 1991.

Bernheim, Kayla. *The Caring Family: Living with Chronic Mental Illness.* N.Y.: Random House, 1982.

Bernheim, Kayla and Anthony Lehman. *Working with Families of the Mentally Ill.* N.Y.: W.W. Norton, 1985.

Bipolar Network News. The Stanley Foundation, 6001 Montrose Road #809, Rockville, MD, 20852. (Free subscriptions: 1-800-518-7326)

Carter, Rosalyn. *Helping Someone with Mental Illness: Compassionate Guide for Family, Friends and Caregivers.* N.Y.: Random House, 1998.

Copeland, Mary Ellen. *The Depression Workbook: A Guide to Living with Depression and Manic Depression.* Oakland, Calif.: New Harbinger Publications, 1992.

DePaulo, Raymond J. *How to Cope with Depression: A Complete Guide for You and Your Family.* N.Y.: McGraw-Hill, 1989.

Duke, Patty and Kenneth Turan. *Call Me Anna.* N.Y.: Bantam Books, 1987.

Duke, Patty, Mary Lou Pinckert, and Gloria Hochman. *A Brilliant Madness: Living with Manic-Depressive Illness.* N.Y.: Bantam Books, 1992.

Gelenberg, A.J. "The Expert Consensus Guideline series: Treatment of bipolar disorder." *Journal of Clinical Psychiatry* 57, Supplement 12A, 1996.

Goodwin, Frederick and Kay Jamison. *Manic-Depressive Illness.* N.Y.: Oxford University Press, 1990.

Group For The Advancement of Psychiatry. *A Family Affair. Helping Families Cope with Mental Illness: A Guide for the Professions.* N.Y.: Brunner/Mazel, 1986.

Hatfield, Agnes. *Coping with Mental Illness in the Family: A Family Guide.* Published 1982. Available from NAMI.

Hatfield, Agnes and Harriet Lefley, eds. *Families of the Mentally Ill: Coping and Adaptation.* N.Y.: Guilford, 1987.

Jamison, Kay. *An Unquiet Mind.* N.Y.: Knopf, 1995.

Johnson, Julie T. *Hidden Victims—Hidden Healers: An Eight Stage Healing Process for Family and Friends of the Mentally Ill.* N.Y.: Doubleday, 1988.

Kanter, Joel. *Coping Strategies for Relatives of the Mentally Ill.* Published 1982. Available from NAMI.

Kaysen, Susanna. *Girl, Interrupted.* N.Y.: Turtle Bay, 1993.

Lefley, Harriet and Mona Wasow. *Helping Families Cope with Mental Illness.* USA: Harwood Publishers, 1994.

McElroy, E. *Children and Adolescents with Mental Illness: A Parents' Guide.* Kensington, Md.: Woodbine House, 1988.

Mondimore, F.M. *Bipolar Disorder: A Guide for Patients and Families.* Baltimore, Md.: Johns Hopkins, 1999.

Moorman, Margaret. *My Sister's Keeper: Learning to Cope with a Sibling's Mental Illness.* N.Y.: W.W. Norton, 1992.

National Depressive and Manic Depressive Association. *Living with Manic Depressive Illness: A Guidebook for Patients, Families and Friends.* National DMDA, 730 N. Franklin Street, Suite 501, Chicago, IL 60610, 1997.

Park, Clara Claiborne. *You Are Not Alone: Understanding and Dealing with Mental Illness: A Guide for Patients, Families, Doctors and Other Professionals.* Boston, Mass.: Little Brown, 1976.

Russell, Mark L. *Planning for the Future: Providing a Meaningful Life for a Child with Disability After Your Death*. Evanston, Ill.: American Publishing Company, 1993.

Schiller, Lori and Amanda Bennett. *The Quiet Room: A Journey Out of the Torment of Madness*. N.Y.: Warren Books, 1994.

Schou, Mogens. *Lithium Treatment of Manic Depressive Illness: A Practical Guide*. N.Y.: Karger, 1989.

Styron, William. *Darkness Visible*. N.Y.: Random House, 1990.

Torrey, E. Fuller, et al. *Schizophrenia and Manic-Depressive Disorder: The Biological Roots of Mental Illness as Revealed by the Landmark Study of Identical Twins*. N.Y.: HarperCollins, 1994.

Vine, Phyllis. *Families in Pain: Children, Siblings, Spouses, and Parents of the Mentally Ill Speak Out*. N.Y.: Pantheon Press, 1982.

Wasow, Mona. *The Skipping Stone: The Rippling Effect of Mental Illness in the Family*. Palo Alto, Calif.: Science & Behavior Books Inc, 1995.

Weiden, Peter J., et al. *Breakthroughs in Antipsychotic Medications: A Guide for Consumers, Families, and Clinicians*. N.Y.: Norton Press, 1999.

Woolis, Rebecca. *When Someone You Love Has a Mental Illness: A Handbook for Family, Friends, and Caregivers*. N.Y.: Putnam, 1992.

Whybrow, Peter. *A Mood Apart: Depression, Mania, and Other Afflictions of the Self*. N.Y.: Harper, 1997.

Zipple, A., S. Langle, L. Spaniol, and H. Fisher. "Client confidentiality and the family's need to know: Strategies for resolving the conflict." *Community Mental Health Journal* 26, no. 6 (1990): 533–545.

FREE MEDICATION PROGRAMS

When I found out about Kristy's disorder, I had no idea medication would cost so much. Luckily, some pharmaceutical companies offer medications for free to families that qualify. All you need is a doctor's consent and proof of your financial status. Family incomes as high as $40,000 annually (offset by expenses, of course) are acceptable by some companies. Below is a list of medications, the corresponding drug companies, and their contact numbers.

Note: Some of these companies may prefer to speak directly with your doctor.

Brand Name	Pharmaceutical Company	Program Phone #
Asendin	Lederle Laboratories	703/706-5933
BuSpar	Bristol-Myers Squibb Company	800/332-2056
Calan	Searle	800/542-2526
Clozaril	Novartis Pharmaceuticals	800/257-3273
Compazine	SmithKline Beecham Pharmaceuticals	800/546-0420
Depakote	Abbott Laboratories	800/441-4987
Desyrel (150 & 300 mg pills only)	Bristol-Myers Squibb Company	800/332-2056

Effexor	Wyeth-Ayerst Laboratories	800/568-9938
Elavil	Zeneca Pharmaceuticals	800/424-3727
Eskalith	Scios, Inc.	800/633-0711
Haldol, Haldol Decanoate	Ortho-McNeil Pharmaceutical, Inc.	800/797-7737
Isoptin	Knoll Pharmaceutical Company	800/524-2474
Klonopin	Roche Laboratories, Inc.	800/285-4484
Lithobid	Solvay Pharmaceuticals, Inc.	800/788-9277
Loxitane	Lederle Laboratories	703/706-5933
Ludiomil	Ciba Pharmaceuticals	800/257-3273
Luvox	Solvay Pharmaceuticals, Inc.	800/788-9277
Navane	Pfizer Inc.	800/646-4455
Norpramin	Hoechst Marion Roussel, Inc.	800/221-4025
Parnate	Scios, Inc.	800/633-0711
Paxil	SmithKline Beecham Pharmaceuticals	800/546-0420
Prolixin, Prolixin Decanoate	Bristol-Myers Squibb Company	800/332-2056
Prozac	Eli Lilly and Company	800/545-6962
Remeron	Organon	800/241-8812
Risperdal	Janssen Pharmaceutica	800/544-2987
Serentil	Boehringer Ingelheim Pharmaceuticals, Inc.	800/556-8317
Serzone	Bristol-Myers Squibb Company	800/332-2056
Sinequan	Pfizer Inc.	800/646-4455
Stelazine	Scios, Inc.	800/633-0711
Surmontil	Wyeth-Ayerst Laboratories	703/706-5933

Tegretol	Novartis Pharmaceuticals	800/257-3273
Thorazine	Scios, Inc.	800/633-0711
Trilafon	Schering Laboratories/Key Pharmaceuticals	800/656-9485
Valium	Roche Laboratories, Inc.	800/285-4484
Wellbutrin	Glaxo Wellcome Inc.	800/722-9294
Zoloft	Pfizer Inc.	800/646-4455
Zyprexa	Eli Lilly and Company	800/545-6962